I DEFY!

Lieut. Dennis Lankford, m.b.e., r.n.v.r.

" *Courage and devotion . . . in the highest traditions of the Service* "

I DEFY!

The story of Lieutenant
DENNIS LANKFORD
M.B.E., R.N.V.R.

presented by
A. Noyes Thomas

LONDON
ALLAN WINGATE

First published in June 1954 by
ALLAN WINGATE (Publishers) Ltd.
12 Beauchamp Place, London SW3

Made and printed in Great Britain by
Metchim & Son Ltd., London

ILLUSTRATIONS

pilots, returning from a sortie, spotted it lying apparently intact in shallow water just off the shore of the mainland, about 100 miles behind the enemy lines.

Other Sea Fury pilots flew off to fix the exact position and, if possible, obtain photographs. It was decided to make an attempt at recovery; at wafting it away under the nose of the enemy. And Captain W. L. M. Brown, commanding the frigate *Cardigan Bay*, was given the tricky task of carrying it off.

The MIG was lying in shoal water. It could be approached only by shallow-draught craft through a tortuous channel in which there were fast-running currents.

So Captain Brown decided to use two junks to which his recovery teams could lash the fighter at low water and then allow the rise of the tide to lift it clear of the sea-bed for towing.

He was about to try this method when he was offered the use of a United States Navy shallow-draught landing craft carrying a mobile crane.

Led by *Cardigan Bay*, the odd little fleet crept up to the mouth of the channel. When it arrived there among the sandbanks, aircraft from *Glory* went roaring away to form a covering screen in case of enemy air attacks; and the cruiser *Kenya*, flying the flag of Rear Admiral A. K. Scott-Moncrieff, who was then Flag Officer Second-in-Command, Far East, hovered around in the middle distance, anxious as a hen about her straying chicks, to give long-range radar cover.

Cardigan Bay then lowered a boat which, guided by one of our Sea Furies, led the landing craft through the shoals to the spot where the MIG lay. Thousands of anxious eyes in *Glory* and the other ships scanned the forbidding coast-line for any sign of activity.

12

As though they were on Margate beach, the recovery teams jumped on to the sandbank and calmly set about fixing slings around the plane. The task could not be completed in one tide, so the ships and boats stayed in their exposed position all night, waiting for the next ebb. It was a dead quiet, whispering night that seemed to last a week.

Soon after dawn the job was completed. The plane was raised and carried away in two parts. A petty officer wearing shallow-water diving gear plunged into the deeper holes recovering various pieces that had broken away.

Then, for good measure, the guns of *Cardigan Bay* and aircraft from the United States carrier *Sicily*, which had arrived on the scene during the darkness, bombarded the enemy coast.

And so, with a lusty roar of cheering, the frigate sailed off with her prize into the Yellow Sea. We heard soon afterwards that the MIG had been sent to Dayton, Ohio, to be stripped of its secrets.

Soon after that I left *Glory* to go on another assignment that promised excitement.

It had been decided that it would be a good idea to send some frigates up to the top end of the Han River estuary, where the waters widen to a kind of lake or lagoon.

The north shore there was in enemy hands and our own front line extended along the southern bank. If a frigate could drop anchor somewhere near the centre and bring her guns to bear on the north bank the Royal Navy would adopt yet another role, that of a " floating front line."

We reckoned that, once there, we could lie at anchor in the lake until the cows came home—or until we ran out of

ammunition—pooping off our guns at enemy troop concen-
trations, ammunition dumps, convoys or any other targets
that offered.

The problem was to get there. And the Australian
frigate *Murchison* went off to see if it was possible. She
tapped her way up the tortuous, unmapped, shoal-studded
channels like a blind woman feeling her way with a stick
along a road that she didn't know. It took her 40 hours to
navigate 30 miles and she made hundreds of soundings.
But she got there.

I humped my cameras aboard the New Zealand frigate
Rotoiti to follow in *Murchison's* footsteps.

We crept along. At first it would have been possible to
pitch a pebble from ship to shore on either side. Then the
channel became wider, but it was studded with grey,
stinking mudbanks.

Our course was marked by buoys that had been dropped
by Murchison, but even so it was tortuous and hard to
follow. And the slightest deviation would have landed us
on the mud to await the next full tide. Stuck fast like
that, we would have been a sitting target for enemy attacks
and probably would have finished up by being blown out of
the water.

It didn't happen. We, too, arrived safely in the lake.
And at once we opened fire.

Every hour on the hour we loosed off with everything we'd
got. Night and day it went on. Mine was a top bunk,
directly below a gun turret. Every sixty minutes throughout every night a salvo would jerk me into a sitting position
and, each time, I would crack my skull on the deckhead.
Soon I was a mass of bruises and abrasions. I began to
wonder who was getting the worst of the bombardment, the
ship's company of *Rotoiti* or the Reds ?

H.M.S. GLORY . . . " She broke most of the records, made 6,400 aircraft launchings." Here is the 4,000th deck landing – and Lieut-Cmdr. F. A. Swanton in his Firefly making it

" In the Yellow Sea . . . pancake ice. At times tugs had to cut a way through "

On the second day I transferred to an old Japanese motor launch operated by the South Korean Navy. It was armed with one Bofors gun for'ard and one Oerlikon trained aft.

The Navigator of *Rotoiti* had invited me to go with him in the little vessel to search for a channel by which the frigates could move closer to the north bank and so bring more targets into range.

While we were taking soundings there was an almighty explosion and a spurt of water a few feet from the side of the launch. We looked towards the shore, saw a puff of smoke, and a mortar bomb crashed through our decking.

We moved rapidly away, but before we were out of range four or five more hits were scored on us. And then *Rotoiti* opened up, plastering the mortar position with four-inch shells. When we had time to take stock we found our only casualty was one South Korean seaman. He had a number of bomb fragments embedded in his back, but it didn't seem to perturb him at all.

In spite of the attack, our navigator had plotted a channel, and next day at high tide the frigate moved along it. As we went, the enemy mortar men ashore, with astonishing temerity, let fly with two rounds—as though to let us know they were still alive. They couldn't have stayed alive for long after that, though. For *Rotoiti's* guns, close up now, promptly blew the whole neighbourhood to pieces. Even the anti-aircraft gunners lent a hand in the operation.

After three days in the lake, all *Rotoiti's* ammunition had gone and as she crept off back to sea I transferred to the frigate *St. Bride's Bay*, which had come to relieve her.

Three more days of shooting and I moved to *Mounts Bay* for another three. All the time I was expecting to have to film an all-out enemy attack on one of the frigates. That was what I was awaiting, but it never came.

15

So back I went to sea while the frigates kept on month after month taking turn and turn about in the lake. On the "rota" was the gallant little *Amethyst*, giving back there far more than she had taken as a prisoner of the Chinese on the Yangtse.

Back at Sasebo I was detailed to accompany Admiral the Hon. Sir Guy Russell, Commander-in-Chief of the Far East Station, on a visit to the Korean front line.

We had arrived at a vantage point overlooking enemy positions when they decided to put down a mortar barrage.

The Admiral went one way—and I went another. I never saw him again.

In a jeep I headed in the direction of Seoul with the idea of making my way to Inchon. I knew the Admiral was due to return there on his way to Yokohama for a meeting with the Americans. But I got caught in a traffic jam. It took me five hours to cover about three miles through a tangle of United Nations transport. Meanwhile (I discovered afterwards), the Admiral had been flown down to Inchon.

When at last I got there he had sailed for Japan. So I joined a tanker that was heading the same way.

Half a day out, we ran into the fringe of a typhoon that had veered unexpectedly in our direction. The 10,000 ton tanker, which was not carrying any cargo and thus rode high in the water, was tossed about like a cockle shell on tremendous seas. It took us three days to complete what should have been a 36-hour passage to Sasebo.

Next I went up to Tokyo, where I stayed for a few days of luxury at the splendid little Maranouchi hotel, run by the Australians primarily for British Commonwealth Officers back from Korea for "rest and recuperation."

16

There I met an old friend of mine from British Pacific Fleet days of World War II, Edward Ward (otherwise Lord Bangor) of B.B.C. broadcast fame.

I mention him because of a remark of his, casually made, that was to have a tremendous significance for me later.

Eddy had been captured during the last war and had spent a lot of time in prisoner-of-war camps. Moreover, he had known China well in the days of the Chiang Kai Shek regime.

Now in the Maranouchi we were talking about the progress of the Korean war and he said :

" I certainly wouldn't like to fall into the hands of these Chinese Communists."

I didn't take much notice at the time. I agreed with him, of course, but quite dispassionately. Wasn't it always some other chap who was captured, poor devil ? It could never be oneself, could it ?

But a day or two later I travelled down to Kure, on the Inland Sea, to rejoin *Murchison* and sail for—captivity.

garbled to the extent that the Chinese imagined a whole United Nations invasion force had come ashore. Otherwise, we argued, why bother . . . why waste all those precious shells ?

Even then we didn't know what was in store for us, but we did appreciate that, at best, we would have to keep an eye on the local population from now on. They would be hopping mad at us for bringing all this wrath down on their little island. We would be very, very unpopular.

It was only about thirty minutes after we had crawled from our funk-holes at the end of the bombardment that we sensed, rather than saw at first, some sort of activity out to sea and just off the beach.

We ran to the edge of a tall cliff and there flopped down on our bellies, with our eyes straining to probe the darkness. And soon we picked it out—a Chinese invasion fleet heading for the shore, the craziest looking collection of flotsam imaginable. There were power-operated junks, sailing junks and junks with outboard motors stuck out over the stern ; there were old barges and power-launches, motorised sampans and dinghies in tow—almost anything that would float, it seemed.

We were too astonished and too fascinated to say anything or do anything. We just lay there watching the infantrymen come streaming ashore—a thousand or more of them, by the look of it. But I think both of us knew at once that we hadn't a cat in hell's chance of giving that little lot the slip on an island two miles long by a mile wide. It just wasn't " on."

We waited for the sound of gunfire, because we knew the islanders had been armed by the Americans for just such an emergency as this. But evidently the local boys had had enough of it, what with bombers and artillery pasting their little place—and now this. Only a few stray shots were fired.

We held a whispered " war conference."

I remembered noticing earlier that a junk lay at anchor in the bay where we had landed and that it had an outboard motor. If we could reach it, the vessel seemed to be our only hope of escape.

So off we went into the darkness, scrambling over the rocks, cursing at every sound we made.

Soon the two of us were trying to burrow into the earth of a slight depression where we had hurled ourselves.

There were voices in the blackness ahead of us. Chinese voices. We were cut off from our junk.

We saw nothing. We could only listen, scarcely daring to breathe. The voices seemed to move away from us. We waited a long time, but they stayed there in the distance.

Inch by inch we crept out of the depression and away. At what we believed was a safer spot, we broke into a run, stumbling and leaping among the rocks, heading for the beach. We thought we might get around the deeply indented coast to our bay.

After six hours of running and walking and crawling around the headland cliffs we were on a narrow ledge about 100 feet above the beach. We found there was no way ahead. And we failed in attempts to climb up or down.

Close behind us, we knew, were the Chinese, for we had heard shouting and the sound of shots. So we couldn't turn back.

Again we tried frantically to scale the cliff above and, this time, we seemed likely to succeed. But just as we

21

The place had no furniture, no furnishings—just mud walls and a mud floor. It was rather like an Eskimo's igloo in shape, with no door and a newspaper stuck over a hole in the wall to admit more light.

Shivering with the sub-zero cold, worrying for all we were worth, the two of us sat in the centre of the floor, huddled together for warmth.

We didn't speak a word. The only move we made was to light up some of the last of our cigarettes. What occupied my companions' mind I don't know, but as for me—I was just waiting to be called outside and shot.

I have no idea why I expected it. I knew well enough that prisoners of war are not, or should not be, treated like that. And usually I have very strong convictions about my future that often seem to work out right in the end. But just at that moment, for some reason, I had quite made up my mind that we were waiting to be called out and shot.

It must have been about midday when at last we were brought out—but not to be bumped off, at least for the moment. We were marched to the top of the highest hill on the island and there we were " introduced " to several Chinamen, who were obviously officers though they had no badges of rank, and to a patently Very Important Person, whom I took to be the Commander of the invasion force.

He ordered us to sit on the hillside and there we squatted for a very long time, feeling hungry, thirsty and frozen to our marrows, gazing wistfully out to sea, where we knew our ships must be.

Every few minutes we appealed for food and drink, having had none so far that day. And at last the V.I.P. relented, ordering one of the soldiers to give us a swig from

24

a water-bottle and a few dry squares that looked and tasted like dog biscuits.

Late in the afternoon, the Chinese seemed to become agitated. And the more agitated they became the higher my hopes soared. I was thinking along the lines of a possible counter-invasion.

Soon, sure enough, scores of vapour trails appeared high in the darkening sky. Our captors covered us with leaves and twigs, and then did the same for themselves. Sabre jets of the United States Air Force came whining down out of the blue, beating up the little island from end to end.

Somehow I felt less lonely, not so hopeless now. Those American aircraft weaving about the sky were friends of mine. They were in this too. And I felt sure their arrival was the prelude to an American invasion.

And now Chinese Air Force MIG fighters came thundering out of the East and the American beat-up developed into a whirl of spectacular dog fights. It ended as suddenly as it had started. And there was silence again.

We had no means of knowing it at the time, or for a very long while afterwards, but all this was really the beginning of what became known as the hundred-day "Battle of the Islands."

The statement about it issued at the time by the Admiralty in London read :—

"For a hundred days ships of the British Commonwealth and United States Navies, assisted by small craft of the Republic of Korea Navy, have fought a 'battle of the islands' off the coasts of Korea.

"Certain of the many islands which lie close to the Korean mainland, principally off the West coast, are of strategic importance to the United Nations forces and the Navy was given the task of retaining them.

" To maintain their day and night guard, the ships of the United Nations Fleets risk critical navigational hazards in the shallow waters of the estuaries and experience constant bad weather at this time of year. They are often under fire from big shore batteries of 105 mm. and 76 mm. mortars and guns. Several ships have been hit, although none seriously, and all have come under fire.

" H.M.S. *Constance* had a two feet diameter hole blown in her plating by the explosion of a shell which hit her above the water-line. H.M.A.S. *Bataan* had her Captain's cabin hit with disastrous results to his best tail-coat.

" The enemy began his push to invade the islands at the end of November. About 1,000 of them came in junks and small boats under covering fire from shore guns and Taewhae-do in the Yalu Gulf fell to them. . . . Left behind there were Lieut. D. A. Lankford R.N.V.R. and Photographer D. Penman who had been ashore to obtain cine and news photographs.

" H.M.S. *Cockade* sank several of the invading junks and one patrol vessel in this action and was herself under fire from the shore batteries.

" Aircraft from the British light fleet carrier *Glory*, the Australian light fleet carrier *Sydney* and the United States light carriers *Badoeng Strait* and *Bairoko* shared the duties of air support and reconnaisance.

" By day, under cover of the big guns of the cruisers, the destroyers and frigates went close inshore to shoot up suspected strong points and hunt out shore batteries. But the batteries were usually mobile and cleverly camouflaged and rarely did the enemy give themselves away to watching aircraft. At night the ships took turns to illuminate the narrow channels between the islands and the mainland with starshells and rocket flares.

"Seamen and Royal Marines from H.M. Ships along with United States and Republic of Korea personnel patrolled in small boats investigating junks and keeping physical contact with the islands at night. Ship's radar swept the seas to locate enemy craft.

"Intense cold and a five-miles-wide track of pancake ice, some large enough to hole a ship, added to the difficulties of the operations. Temperatures fell to as low as 9 degrees Fahrenheit. At times tugs had to cut a way through the ice for the warships to proceed."

Neither hearing nor seeing any more of the intense sea and air activity there must have been at that time in that area, we lay, cold as all creation, on the hillside until perhaps one o'clock next morning. Later I got used to the almost incredibly low temperature, but now it struck unmercifully into my vitals.

At last we were told to get up and were embarked in a sailing junk. A mile or so out to sea we were transferred to an old Japanese motor-launch and battened down in the evil-smelling hold, which seemed to be full of rifles and bloodstained clothing.

It puzzled us at the time. Later we discovered that, however expendable the Chinese soldier may be, his clothing and equipment are greatly valued. Here, in the hold with us, was the sickening aftermath of battle—the material saved from some suicidal onslaught.

We had no idea where we were going. So far, no one had spoken to us in English. We could only guess. And when at last we were taken ashore in a sampan we guessed, rightly as it turned out, that we were on the mainland of North Korea, far behind the enemy lines.

Joining us now in captivity was a Korean civilian doctor. We gathered that he, too, had been brought from our island. But he spoke not a word. Immediately the three of us set off with a strong escort on a ten-mile cross-country march, after which we were met by some more Chinese soldiers with an open truck.

At once the Korean doctor was bound tightly with ropes. As we watched we felt sure that this was where we were to face the firing party. But no.

Into the truck we were bundled for a three-hour drive to a small Korean village, where an English-speaking Chinaman met us.

As we staggered from the truck he assured us that we had been " liberated from Imperialism, the highest form of Capitalism." He added his hope that very soon we would study hard and join the ranks of the peace-loving peoples of the world to strike a heavy blow at our old employers, the warmongers.

I don't know why I remember his words. I hardly heard them at the time, I was so numbed by cold and racked with hunger. Perhaps they have stuck in my memory because they were so ridiculous in the circumstances, so very untimely.

Nevertheless I am grateful to that man, for he led us to our first meal—a bowl of boiled rice, some decomposing dried fish and hot water to drink. I could hardly get it down, but many times during the months that followed I would have trudged any number of miles for such a feast.

We spent that night in the village at a house from which the inhabitants departed readily enough after the soldiers had offered them spot-cash payment. I noticed many times afterwards that the Chinese, in their dealings with North Koreans, were always meticulous in this matter of providing prompt compensation for displacement, and in paying for any services rendered or goods received.

Early next morning the English-speaking Chinaman reappeared and told us :

" You will now walk to another place."

" Where to, and how far away ? " I asked.

" About two miles away," he replied.

It was always to " another place " with these Chinamen and, as I was to discover, it was always " about two miles away."

After seven hours of marching we arrived at what was obviously a Chinese divisional headquarters, set up in the mud huts of a village. There the Korean doctor, still tightly bound, was taken away. I never saw him again. He had not uttered one word since the moment we encountered him, so we had no idea why he had been taken prisoner. But I often wonder about the poor devil's fate.

Now, through an interpreter, we were asked to give our names, our units and our ranks. These were legitimate questions and we replied truthfully.

Then our interrogator, who seemed to be a fairly high ranking officer, let off a little speech in Chinese. The interpreter translated :

" Our comrade says he is pleased to note your co-operative attitude. Our comrade wishes you to know that you must consider yourselves not to have been captured but to have been liberated by the Chinese People's Volunteers. Our comrade says further that very soon you will be taken to a rear area, where you will be safe from the bombings of the capitalist warmongers."

By now we were becoming thoroughly exhausted, mentally and physically. We had hoped that we might remain where we were for that night, but the interpreter said :

"You will now go to another place. There you will have a comfortable room. It is about two miles away."

After about an hour and a half of hard marching we reached a Korean farmhouse and were shut in a room which, mercifully, contained a glowing *habachi*, or little charcoal-burning stove without a chimney, rather like a miniature brazier.

We felt well rested when we were awakened in the morning for a hot meal of plain boiled rice, and a watery soup with long, black things like bootlaces floating in it. They had no taste, were of the consistency of rubber and, I learned later, were made from dried soya bean curd.

For most of that day I was asked questions. How long had I served ? When had I arrived in Korea ? Why had I come to Korea ?

To this last one I found myself answering : "To fight Communism." The Chinese tried to smile—a little grimly, I thought. But I was tired, dejected and furious about my position. I couldn't resist the temptation to say what I believed.

Apparently my impertinence was not held against me though no doubt it was noted down and may have contributed towards bringing about my later misfortunes. But up to now the Chinese were being scrupulously correct.

For two days we waited there for transport to take us to "another place." We couldn't discover where we were going, except that it was somewhere up near the border of Korea and Manchuria.

At last a truck arrived—an open, Russian-made one—and we set out on a long, bitter, two-day ride at breakneck speed over winding, mountain roads, through snow and ice, stopping overnight *en route* at a lonely Korean house from which, again, the inhabitants were paid to get out.

It was very late in the following afternoon when we reached our destination, which turned out to be Pyoktong, at that time the main prisoner-of-war camp in North Korea for non-Asiatic United Nations personnel.

We didn't enter the camp at once. That night we were kept in a hut on the outskirts of the township and there filled out P.O.W. registration forms which, in theory, should have got back to the United Nations Command in South Korea, but in my case never did.

Next day, my companion was taken away and I entered the gaol where, as I had already been informed, I was to be the only British officer.

By then, all the prisoners had been deprived of their uniforms and were wearing blue quilted jackets and trousers similar in shape to those of the Chinese soldiers. The sudden appearance among them of a lieutenant of the Royal Navy rigged out complete with cap at the proper, jaunty angle, seemed to cause quite a stir.

CHAPTER THREE

THE CAMP AT Pyoktong consisted of part of the township from which the inhabitants had been evacuated. It lay at the end of a peninsula that jutted out into a great natural reservoir. And the bare, brown mud huts that we occupied were situated on the gentle slopes rising from a shallow valley that ran the length of the headland.

In almost every way this gaol of ours was unlike the general conception of such a place. There was no suggestion of orderliness about it; no lines of brick or wooden hut-ments. There were no great barricades of barbed wire; no encircling walls or fences; no batteries of searchlights or guns.

Security was provided simply by the water (or the ice in winter) that hemmed it in on three sides; by the scores of sentries and by constant patrols. And how effective these arrangements were is proved by the fact that no-one, as far as I know, ever succeeded in escaping, though many tried.

It was mid-winter when I arrived there and I noticed at once that, although the nights were long, the darkness was never deep. Even in cloudy conditions, or when there was no moonlight, a certain amount of light seemed to be reflected from the great expanse of ice. Anyone trying to move across it would have been discernible even from a considerable distance.

And there were many other major obstacles in the path of the would-be escapee—as I discovered from my fellow prisoners within a very few hours. For one thing there was the near impossibility of securing any food with which to sustain life in that frozen, snow-bound world. Then there was the bitter, active hostility and hatred of 11,000,000 bombed and battered North Koreans with which to cope— not to mention the watchfulness of a couple of million Chinese soldiers swarming over the countryside. And there was the obvious difficulty for a Westerner of merging among Oriental peoples with their distinctive build and features, exotic ways and peculiar, quite inimitable gait.

On my arrival I was shown to one of the igloo-like mud huts that was occupied already by eight Americans. It was completely bare and so small that it was impossible for all of us to sleep on the floor at the same time.

The Americans greeted me with remarkable warmth, considering that my presence would represent a tricky added problem to their domestic arrangements. Fortunately, however, they were old lags by now, and had their life well organised.

At night, for instance, we would take it in turns to lie down full length on the floor for a few hours' sleep while some sat hunched like gnomes in the corners, or simply stood up.

Our chief joy was the warmth with which we were provided. It came from a somewhat decrepit version of one of the world's most ancient forms of central heating, a system that has been in use in Korea for centuries and which, I have often thought, might with advantage be adapted to improve the winter-time amenities of many a chilly British abode.

It worked like this. Outside the hut there was a deep hole leading to a tunnel which passed under the mud floor and came out into a chimney built into the wall on the other side. When a wood fire was lighted in the hole, the heat was drawn under the length of the floor and up into the chimney, thus warming the whole place.

Unfortunately, our hut appeared to be an old one. The mud floor was cracked and crumbling, so that at times smoke belched out of the ground, almost suffocating us. Several times each night the alarm would be raised and we would all turn out, spluttering and coughing, while a new leak in the earth was sealed.

Nevertheless, our affection for that heating system was deep and sincere. We nursed it along tenderly, always fearful lest—as sometimes happened when fuel ran short— it should die out and leave us to lie shivering on the cold earth in 30 degrees or so of frost.

Judging by what I have heard of prison-camps in other wars and other countries, our treatment under the Chinese at Pyoktong was not harsh. For instance, we were never made to do any work except that which was directly to our own advantage, such as cooking, chopping firewood or unloading our own supplies. And there was little regimentation.

At dawn each day our guards would awaken us for roll-call by clanging together two great lumps of iron. With that check completed, we would of our own accord make attempts at ablutions, in which we used old United States Army steel helmets to serve as basins.

Breakfast in our huts came at 9.30. It consisted always of boiled rice and a stew containing a few unpeeled potatoes, some cabbage leaves and a Japanese vegetable called dikon, which seemed to be a cross between a radish and a turnip.

At 10 a.m. while I was in the camp (I heard that this part of the programme was dropped after I had been taken away for " interrogation ") there was a lecture from an English-speaking Chinaman. Usually the subject matter was some aspect of Communism, or the Chinese viewpoint of progress in the Korean war. It was at one of these sessions that I was first informed I should regard myself not only as having been " liberated " rather than " captured," but also as being a " student " rather than a prisoner.

Returning to out huts at about 11 a.m. we were required to discuss between ourselves, with our own squad leader as a chairman, what we had just heard and then to write individual essays, expressing our own views on the subject. These literary efforts would then be taken to Camp H.Q., marked like school lessons, and eventually placed in the personal file that the Chinese kept for each of us.

We treated the whole thing with the light-heartedness and contempt that it seemed at the time to deserve. Just what used to be written down on some of the sheets of doled-out paper I shudder to think. For myself, not dreaming what lay ahead of me, I passed the time by trying to be as facetious and to write in as much *double-entente* as possible. If in fact the file containing those essays did follow me about on my subsequent journeyings in captivity, and if the contents were taken seriously by my humourless captors, it could well be that I paid dearly in toil, tears and torture for those few hours of what seemed to be comparatively innocent amusement.

After the essay session, there being no mid-day meal, the hours from about noon until 4 p.m. were designated a

" period of recreation." During that time, some of us just stood or sat around talking. Some went visiting at neighbouring huts. Some played poker or other games with battered decks of home-made cards, or chess with sets beautifully hand-carved from firewood.

Others, more energetic, went in for basket-ball, soft-ball, volley-ball and, very occasionally, British soccer or American football. At the two latter games we did our best, but really the available flat space was too small and the ground too rocky and too frozen for football of any kind. Attempts to play it were farcical, if not downright dangerous.

At 4 p.m. came the second and final meal of the day. Usually it brought a repetition of the breakfast menu, but sometimes we would be given also some unappetising scrap, perhaps the eyeball of a Korean hog, an animal that looks like no other pig I have ever seen. It lives by scrounging among the night-soil and other filth of the towns and villages and appears to carry no lean flesh whatsoever.

It was gruesome for a newcomer to the camp to watch a prisoner trying to swop some revolting portion of carcass for another morsel he considered more palatable. At first I could not face the meat at all. I tried and was sick. After a few days I managed to swallow some of it and keep it down. Soon it was to seem almost a delicacy.

Darkness came at about 5 p.m., soon after we had finished the meal. Then we would lie down, or squat in a corner if it was our turn to sleep later. For a while we would talk, chiefly of the past and little of the present. One by one we would doze off to sleep and quiet—silence deeper than any I had experienced up to that time—would enfold the camp.

Towards the end of my brief stay at Pyoktong—my only experience of an ordinary prisoner-of-war camp during the twenty-three months I was to spend in captivity—came

Christmas day. I must describe it here because it fell just forty-eight hours before I was plucked from the camp for the beginning of my inquisition, and because the contrast with what was to follow was so remarkable.

We tried our best to keep it in traditional fashion and the Chinese seemed quite ready to help us, within reason, to do so. In fact they went to great pains to assure us that they did not propose to interfere in any way with whatever religious occasions we saw fit to celebrate.

At our request they provided us with some coloured paper and a few boxes of children's paints to use in making decorations. Among us were some skilled artists who quickly produced gaily coloured placards bearing such messages as "Peace on Earth, Goodwill toward Men," "Merry Christmas," "A Happy New Year," "Peace in 1952."

There was no shortage of fir branches from the saplings growing in profusion on the hillsides and we even managed to produce a few sprigs of holly and mistletoe.

So every hut was decorated, inside and out, in our bid to recapture the spirit of happier Christmases past. With cold, soggy rice as an adhesive, we pasted the paper decorations on to mud walls, doors and wooden posts. We made little lanterns from paper and cardboard, using stubs of candles to light them. We improvised arches from fir branches.

And to complete the Yuletide picture, there was a fresh fall of snow on Christmas Eve so that, the following morning, it lay on the ground deep and crisp and even. As we emerged from our huts at dawn to gaze out on the landscape, there must have been a lump in many a throat, for our gaol nestling among the frosty firs now resembled so closely the scenes on Christmas cards that would not be reaching us—this year.

Early in the morning, choirs of carol singers toured the huts, as they had done in the darkness of the previous evening. I was a member of one group of choristers, and I shall never forget the sight of grown men with tears trickling down their faces as they listened to our rendering of " Silent Night, Holy Night." I shall always remember the spine-tingling warmth and sincerity of the singing. And I shall never again hear a carol without thinking back to the quiet, unspoken welcome we received from the sick and wounded prisoners lying on the bare mud floor of the shack that served as a hospital. Many of them, I know, were thinking how unlikely it was that they would see, ever again, a Christmas in their own homes and among their own folk. Some, I suspect, were hoping not to see even another day, such were their sufferings and their states of mind. A few obviously were dying.

After the carols came religious services, first for Protestants and then for Catholics. There were no Padres in the camp, but nevertheless we did our best, with altars improvised from packing cases and rough crosses fashioned from odd bits of wood. And again the Chinese helped out by providing a few fat candles to complete the effect.

Amost everyone, regardless of denomination, attended both services. The atmosphere at each was electric. But whether this arose chiefly from religious fervour aroused by the poignancy of our situation, or whether it resulted from the thoughts of home and of Christmasses past that the occasion brought to mind is something I shall never be able to decide. But certainly to my own mind the special prayers, filled as they were with hopes of peace, freedom and repatriation in the following year, brought—I think for the

38

first time fully—frightful anxieties as to whether my parents in London would ever come to know that I was a prisoner and was not dead and whether I would live to see them again.

After the services we staged a short but—so it seemed to us—touchingly enacted Nativity play. And then there was a variety concert.

All this time our Chinese guards, most of whom had never had any first-hand contact with Western Christmas festivities, hung around watching, perfectly impassive, but obviously intrigued just the same. The better educated among them tried to feign a certain disinterest, but the peasant types were hanging on every word and every movement.

The Chinese officers did not seem to realise it, but months of their work on attempts at Communist indoctrination went to the winds that Christmas day, not that their efforts ever showed any real signs of success in that camp.

For Christmas dinner, which we ate in the late afternoon, we were given as extras some chickens and a couple of very good pigs between the 1,500 or so of us. We also had a handful each of peanuts and some boiled sweets, all brought specially for the occasion from China by barge.

Each man then received a shot of Soju, a spirit made from rice, very strong to the taste and extremely potent. Its effect on some of the men who had spent a long time in captivity was disastrous. Even the one ration of the stuff made some of them tipsy, but there were many who, by barter and by other means, did not have to stop at one.

Our next surprise was an issue of tea—Chinese green tea, it was, but tea nonetheless.

"You will now write your confession. You will admit that you are a spy, a saboteur and an agent—a war criminal. You will sign what you write and then throw yourself on the mercy of the peace-loving peoples of the world."

He paused, then added: "If you choose to be a peace fighter and will study Communism seriously, with a view to embracing it, no harm will come to you."

Both the men looked at me. The interrogator, I remember thinking, was quite handsome in an Oriental way. But just at that moment he seemed to me to have a particularly evil expression.

"I've nothing to confess," I protested. "Your accusations are ridiculous."

I was about to explain my Navy job, to say that I was Fleet Naval Information Officer, and dealt only in providing newsreel and Press pictures of the Navy, but I had no chance to say more.

The interrogator spoke and the interpreter translated just one word :

"Write."

The two stalked off, leaving me with my own thoughts.

I realised clearly enough that the Chinese intended to make it tough for me if I refused to do as I was told. And I imagined that, even if I made a false confession to placate them, I would probably be making out my own death warrant. I seemed to remember reading something about the Geneva convention authorising the execution of prisoners proved to be spies. But how I wished I knew more about the thing.

In the evening the interrogator and interpreter returned. They saw that the paper they had left with me was still blank. They told me that by continuing to refuse to

" co-operate " I would " destroy my own future." **They** used the phrase again and again, and each time I liked **the** sound of it less.

All through the night they talked at me. " Write," they would say, and each time I would reply : " I will not." " Co-operate, or you will destroy your own future " . . . " I will not write." The ritual seemed to go on endlessly.

At dawn the piece of paper was still lying in front of me— still blank. And then the interpreter said he would take me for a walk. " I think you need some exercise," he said.

The thought crossed my mind that this might be my last walk, and yet somehow I felt convinced I wasn't going to die just yet. It is difficult not to make it sound melo-dramatic, but curiously enough I didn't feel particularly worried. I didn't seem to care whether this chap was going to bump me off or not. In fact I seemed almost to have persuaded myself that a bullet in the back might save me a hell of a lot of trouble.

Over the snow the two of us walked, away from the town and into the fir-clad hills. I thought of making a dash for freedom, but realised that without even a proper escape plan it would be suicidal—that I would be recaptured at once, or else die of cold and hunger.

The interpreter talked to me quietly all the time. He said he wanted to be friends, that it was silly of me not to confess, as I was bringing only trouble on my own head— which was the last thing he wanted to see.

" Let's not have any nastiness. Let's all be happy." That was his line.

On our return after two hours, he gave me a hot meal of rice and to my amazement—scrambled eggs. I asked for

43

Not on your life !

And with that firm conviction I lay down on the ground and fell fast asleep. I noticed often during my captivity that at intervals between the crises, when my mind was in a whirl of fears and doubts, I would fall off blissfully to sleep. It was as though nature stepped in to soothe and refresh a mind in torment.

At dawn the inquisitors returned. They examined the sheets of paper and, finding them blank, became very angry.

" You will now be given your last chance." The interpreter echoed in English the high-pitched Chinese words of the interrogator. " You will be given the whole of the next two days to write a self-criticism and confess sincerely to the Chinese People's Volunteers. You will end by writing that, if you are found to have been insincere, you will gladly accept any punishment that the C.P.V. may decide to inflict upon you."

Again I was left alone. For two whole days I saw no one except the guard who brought me food in the mornings and evenings—good food it was, too, by prison standards.

I began to think they had decided to leave me be, but on the third day at dawn back they came, like two bad, yellow pennies.

They found me asleep, and obviously were cross about it. They discovered the paper was still blank, and became really excited over that.

" You must prepare for trouble," they told me. " If it becomes necessary to shoot you and your own side accuses us of having murdered a prisoner, our reply will be that, in our opinion after gathering conclusive evidence, you were a spy, a saboteur, and that according to the Geneva Convention we were within our rights in disposing of you."

They went on to say that, between them and me, they would be prepared to have me shot at any moment, with or without evidence about my being a spy. And with the next breath they were explaining that, of course, they wouldn't really have me shot at all, as that was not the way in which the new people of the new China, the Chinese People's Volunteers or the peace-loving peoples of the world behaved.

They would . . . They wouldn't. The situation was becoming as clear as mud.

I'll never know why, but for some reason the threats at that stage had no effect on me whatever. I was not afraid. I wasn't even particularly worried. I felt nothing, except that perhaps I was becoming rather cocky. I think my attitude was : " If there's going to be some shooting, let's have it now."

Next my Chinamen brought me two books—a textbook on Communism in U.S.S.R. and a philosophic treatise by Mao Tse Tung, the Red leader of China, called " On Practice." They also handed over a few very old copies of the London " Daily Worker."

There was nothing else to do, nothing else even to look at, so I read the lot. They didn't interest me. They didn't bore me. I read, and then read again. The mechanical process of following the printed lines seemed to occupy my mind, seemed to make the time pass. At the end of a page I would barely know what it contained.

Again, after a time, I began to think that perhaps I was to be left alone. But again the two Chinamen returned.

At last, with blows raining on me, I crawled to a corner, forced myself into a sitting position and stayed there, propped against the two walls.

I tried to ward off the blows. I tried to shut my ears to all the threats of what would happen if I didn't obey orders and stand up.

The truth was that I couldn't stand up. I had neither the will, nor the strength. All I wanted was to be put out of my misery.

They dragged me to my feet. I fell against the wall but, miraculously, my knees did not buckle. I stayed like that for what seemed an eternity—until dawn, in fact. Then they let me sit on the floor.

" *You will crack before we do*," the interpreter told me again and again. " Why not save yourself unnecessary anguish ? "

All that day, with brief intervals of squatting on the floor, I was made to stand, always with a bludgeon held ready by my guard to send me crashing to the ground and another to drive me to my feet again.

" *You will crack before we do*," I heard the words again.

And this time I summoned the strength to make a very rude sign at my tormentors.

They didn't miss it. They demanded that I should explain what it meant. Squatting on my haunches, bruised, bleeding, on the verge of collapse, I did so—in great detail and in words that are quite unprintable.

They waited for the end of my tirade. I expected them to fly into a frenzy of fury. But they didn't. For a moment I thought I hadn't been sufficiently clear as to my meaning— until I was told :

" You have committed yet another crime. You have insulted the Chinese People's Volunteers, the representatives of the peace-loving peoples of the world. You will pay the price."

I toyed with the idea of trying to bang their silly heads together, but I knew I hadn't the strength. In any case, the guards would have shot me dead before I could have reached my tormentors. Many times afterwards, I looked back on that time and wished I had tried—with the inevitable result.

After that outburst I was left to myself again for some days—the idea presumably being that I would ponder over what " price " I might have to pay.

But that night I slept soundly again.

It was about three weeks after the beginning of the attempts to make me sign a confession that the Chinese tried a new line of approach.

They brought me a confession already drawn up and told me to sign it. I refused even to look at the thing.

The interrogator and translator left the room without a word and as they went, in came two hefty Chinese soldiers whom I hadn't seen before.

They closed the door behind them and, while one covered me with a sub-machine gun, the other took off his coat and, to my amazement, began squaring up to me like a boxer opening a bout.

I couldn't be sure what his game was and I let him strike the first blow without trying even to dodge it.

That did it. I am rather hot-tempered at the best of times and now that stunning blow brought all the fury of days of injustice and bitterness boiling up in my veins.

CHAPTER FIVE

AFTER THE "BIG fight," the Chinese left me alone. They didn't subject me to any more interrogation and the bullying stopped. My meals arrived regularly, night and morning. I spent my time pacing about the hut, first one way and then another. There was nothing else to do. I couldn't sleep *all* the time.

It was the old Chinese game, of course. They knew they had got me worked up—frightened. So they left me there, alone day after day, hoping I would worry myself sick over what might happen next.

Once one of the English-speaking Chinamen did put his head inside the doorway to enquire :

" You all right ? "

" Oh, sure," I replied sarcastically, " I'm fine. Couldn't be better. Having a wonderful time."

And I added quickly : " Look here, what the hell was the idea of turning that crazy pug of yours loose on me ? "

" Pug ? Crazy ? I turn him loose," he answered blandly, shrugging his shoulders as though he had not understood me.

Then he said : " If you mean to ask why it was necessary for one of the guards to strike you, then I will reply that it was so because of your ungrateful, cowardly attack on him.

You should consider yourself fortunate that you have not been punished for assaulting one of the Chinese People's Volunteers. It is not good, it is not wise to act as you have acted."

I heard him out and then made a single retort : " Balderdash," or a word to that effect.

He ignored the expletive.

" Now," he went on " you will be left to yourself to think over your attitude. When you have decided to be reasonable—to sign the confession, you will ask your guard to fetch me and I will come to see you."

" Chummy," I replied, " you might just as well nip off back to China and get on with your farming. You won't be hearing from me."

He looked at me steadily for a long time. Perhaps he recognised from my attitude that I had reached, in my mental appreciation of my situation, a stage where I realised it was no good even pretending to be polite any more ; that I had nothing to lose ; that I might just as well let them know how I felt.

He shook his head as though he was genuinely sad for me. And then he said softly :

" We think you are quite idiotic that you should try to stand up for a cause that so obviously is lost."

He left me wondering what he meant. Perhaps he was referring to the United Nations, but I suspected strongly that the " lost cause " must be me.

I didn't spend long worrying about that, though. I was too busy, now, planning out the details of the escape bid which I had decided quite definitely to make without delay. I was as excited as a schoolboy on the last day of term. I made up my mind to head by the shortest route for

55

the west coast of North Korea. I couldn't think how far that might be, but from what I remembered of talk in the P.O.W. camp, I knew it must be nearer than the east coast and probably both nearer and easier to reach than our own front line to the south.

On the shore of the Yellow Sea I hoped to steal a boat of some kind, perhaps a small junk, in which to sail south, across the 38th Parallel, into more friendly waters.

Maybe, I told myself, I would be spotted by one of the United Nations aircraft which, I knew well, always flew low to investigate any small craft seen off the coast. Or maybe I would be picked up by one of the many United Nations ships that were patrolling ceaselessly in the West Coast area.

There were difficulties and dangers about which I scarcely dared to think. But I knew I must plan against them if I was to have any chance at all of success.

For one thing I would have to keep away from populated areas. It was hopeless to think of trekking overland in daylight among Oriental peoples, with their inimitable appearance and strange gait. Among them I could not hope to avoid instant detection.

Then there was the handicap of my ignorance of the geography of this part of the country. I could " navigate " by the stars, but what if there weren't any stars to be seen ? I knew I stood the risk of becoming hopelessly lost in that white wilderness and dying of exposure and hunger.

Hunger—that raised another issue. During winter the fields lay buried deep beneath snow, so there would be no hope of stealing food from growing crops. And I would not dare approach any human habitation. The North Koreans, incensed by the shattering air raids to which they had been subjected, no doubt would tear me to pieces, lynch me if they got their hands on me.

It was while I was pondering over these depressing facts—somewhere about the end of January I think it must have been—that I had a great piece of good fortune.

One morning, while visiting the latrine which lay about thirty paces across the snow from my hut, I saw a very ragged Korean boy, probably about twelve years old, who seemed to be hiding behind a pile of logs.

I wouldn't have taken much notice of him, as little war waifs always hung around hoping for scraps of food at any place where Chinese soldiers were stationed. But to my astonishment this lad gave me a big smile, stuck two grubby thumbs in the air and said : " Americano, O.K."

I returned the greeting with a slight wave of the hand across my face, taking care that my guards did not notice it.

Back in my hut, I was filled with a wild joy. Here was a friend in my loneliness. Here, perhaps, was the key to my escape.

I argued with myself that the main reason for the failure of so many bids for freedom by United Nations prisoners in North Korea was that none of those other chaps had received any help from the civilian population, and so had never been able to get enough food.

But in this boy, surely, there was the ghost of a chance. If I could persuade him to accompany me, he might be able to procure food along the way by begging or stealing. He might have some knowledge of local geography. And probably he would be able to show me the tricks of survival in these near-Arctic conditions.

It seemed wildly improbable that the child would have anything to do with my scheme. After all, he had only smiled, stuck his thumbs in the air and said a three-word greeting. And here I was expecting the earth of him, and pinning all my hopes on him.

But he was my straw, and I was clutching as desperately as any drowning man.

That day I explained in sign language to my guard that I was suffering from dysentry and would have to make frequent visits to the latrines. And I went out four or five times during the day, as often as I dared.

The last time it was just getting dark and I was losing hope when I spotted the lad hiding behind the pile of logs again.

By mime I tried to make him understand that I wanted to vamoose, buzz off. I indicated that I wished him to come with me and to get food for me. I pointed to his eyes to tell him he should use them to guide me. Quickly I got over to him the idea that he should wait in hiding the next morning at the same spot.

He nodded his head up and down several times and then seemed to melt into the gathering gloom.

That night I didn't sleep at all, I was so excited. I had no intention of slipping away next day, but wanted to establish the lad's sincerity. If he kept the appointment, at least it would be some small guarantee of good faith.

Next morning I made several more visits to the toilet. During one of these, at about noon, I sensed the lad was somewhere about, but couldn't see him.

Here I should explain that the latrine consisted simply of a deep, narrow trench with two tree trunks lying horizontally along it.

Suddenly I heard a rustle and looked sharply to the right. And there, further along the trench, was the Korean lad, the top of his head just level with the logs, his feet balanced on two rocks, among the filth at the bottom of the excavation.

We smiled at one another, but didn't speak a word. Using mime again, I pointed to the sun, traced its passage twice across the sky and gave him the idea that I wanted him to meet me in the darkness after two more full days.

He pointed to the top of a hill nearby and I understood that our rendezvous should be there.

I had plumped for an inverval of two more days because, even now, I wanted a little more time to think, and because I feared the guard had begun to suspect my tale of dysentry was untrue.

Now I was in a fever of excitement, going over and over in my mind the best means of leaving my mud hut without detection.

It had only one door, outside which a guard stood night and day. But on one of the other walls there was an 18-inch hole covered by a sheet of newspaper—a typical Korean window.

I decided that if I eased off the newspaper where it was stuck to the wall at the lower end I could slip through the hole and then pull the covering back into position so that, from the outside, there would be no sign of anything amiss.

I realised that the guards very seldom put their heads around the door once they had closed it behind me. I knew that there was only one guard on duty at a time. And I was certain that he usually remained in a position, leaning against an animal fodder trough, from which he could not see the window.

At about 1 a.m. on the appointed night I eased the paper from the wall. Then I clambered through the hole head first, landing on my hands, and gently pulled the covering back into position.

This last manoeuvre made a tiny sound, but it was loud as gunfire to me. I didn't wait to see the effect but ran off on tip-toe as fast as I could go, scarcely noticing the steep gradient of the hillside.

A few small stones were dislodged by my boots and went rolling down into the valley. But either my guard was asleep or he was too far away to hear. Perhaps the noise was deadened by the snow. Anyway there was no challenge.

By the time I had reached the crest of the hill, where there were a few scraggy trees, my nerves were completely on edge. I jumped at the slightest sound.

And I nearly shouted out when a tiny figure darted from behind a tree trunk and tugged quickly at my sleeve. It was the Korean lad—Kim, I called him. He had kept his word.

It was then that we spoke to one another for the first time apart from that first greeting, " Americano . . . O.K." I found that besides Korean, he understood a little Chinese, some Japanese, and surprisingly in North Korea, a few words of pidgin-English.

I tried to make him understand that I wanted to get away as quickly as possible from the reservoir area where my hut stood and to meet the west-flowing Yalu River. I shall never know whether he really got the idea, but off we went.

Mercifully, it was snowing gently, so that our tracks were covered almost as soon as we had made them. And a great morale booster came by courtesy of the Chinese People's Volunteers. Their quilted prison suit was blue on the outside, but white inside. By turning it inside out, I had the perfect camouflage for this icy new world of mine.

Kim led me away from the immediate camp area by what seemed a crazily roundabout route. Every now and then he would stop, put a finger to his lips in an appeal for silence and then point in one direction saying "Chungwa." The word meant "Chinese" and I assumed he was telling me of small outposts we were skirting.

The country was wild and rugged. It looked as though at some time there might have been some fearful subterranean upheaval that had left the surface of the earth in a mad confusion of narrow valleys and jagged, untidy hills rising to 1,000 or 1,500 feet. Some of the valleys were so hemmed in that they were little more than crevices. Some of the hills were bare of vegetation and others were thickly wooded with firs. The surface everywhere was treacherous. About nine inches of snow covered loose, crumbling rock that I would have expected, in that climate, to have been frozen into one rigid mass, but which came away frequently under my feet, sending me stumbling, or crashing, to the ground.

But I could put up with that, if only the snow continued, as it was doing still, to fall gently and cover our tracks.

For all our hurrying, I don't suppose we covered more than five miles that night.

Just before first light we found a hiding place among some rocks on high ground and there settled down to wait for darkness again.

Sleep was impossible. My nerves were much too taut: I was too excited. From our vantage point I saw several groups of Chinese soldiers moving about the lower ground, apparently searching for me. But no one came near.

Our chances of being discovered there were pretty remote, I thought, but I worked out a route by which we might slip away—just in case.

As soon as the sun had set we were off again, heading in the direction of the last faint glow in the western sky, making for the mighty Yalu River.

We seemed to be in a silent, frozen world of nothingness. We didn't see a single house. We didn't see even an animal of any kind.

There were only the birds by day to keep us company—magpies with their black and white plumage gleaming in the sunshine, huge crows and cocky little sparrows. I rejoiced in the utter loneliness of it.

Now we were down on the ice of the reservoir. The coating of snow provided a grip for our feet and we half skated, half ran along at a good speed.

Finally, just before the second dawn, we came to the end of an arm of the reservoir, climbed a hill and looked down the other side to see the Yalu—my path to freedom.

We found another hiding place for the daylight hours. Kim, after saying something like " Needy chopa, chopa ? " from which I gathered he meant did I want food, slipped off. I presumed he had gone to get some, though I couldn't imagine where.

Moving along during the nights it had seemed warm enough, even though I knew the temperature must have been far below freezing, perhaps as much as 30 degrees below.

During the days in hiding I scooped snow away with my hands and then lay in the depression, protected from the cruel wind but warmed slightly by the sun.

I made a snug little bed for myself after Kim had slipped away, but as soon as I lay down in it doubts crept into my mind.

Had the lad really gone off to find food in this white wilderness ? Or had he gone to some Korean police post of which he knew, there to report finding an escaped prisoner and so, perhaps, win some kind of reward ?

Was the child really a friend ? Or was he up to some treachery ? I couldn't make up my mind.

All I knew about him was what he had tried to tell me during our flights by night : that he hated the Chinese. His widowed mother, apparently, had refused to let her mud hut home be requisitioned by them. She had thrown out the soldiers' packs and they had informed the Korean police, who had carried her off to prison leaving the lad to find for himself. Now he was trying to get his revenge by helping me.

All he could know about me was that I was not an " Americano," as he had thought at first ; that I was just another of the enemies who were raking his homeland from end to end with fire and fury.

In a torment of doubt I decided to move from my hiding place and go to another about 500 yards away from which I could see if Kim returned alone. If he didn't, I would run for it, even in daylight.

There—tired, hungry, cold and bewildered—I fell fast asleep.

When I awoke the sun was low and there was no sign of Kim. I rushed across to the old hiding place, dreading that he might have returned to it and, not finding me there, gone away in fright.

But there he was in the hollow, sleeping blissfully. Poor lad, he must have had doubts about me as deep as mine had been about him.

Beside him, in a paper bundle, was some food which I ate greedily. But when he awakened at sunset and smiled confidently at the sight of my bearded face I wondered, for the first time, whether I had eaten his share too.

When I tried to apologise he assured me that he had been to some lonely farmhouse and had been given a good feed, some of which he had secreted away for me.

We laughed heartily. The food and sleep had given us new strength.

We scrambled down the hillside to the ice of our river, which must have been about three-quarters of a mile wide at that point and was completely frozen over. Turning left, we struck towards the sea, which I thought to be about 45 miles downstream.

Somehow Kim seemed to know the exact position of dams, power stations, anti-aircraft emplacements and other places likely to be guarded. As we approached them we made wide detours, thus adding considerably to the mileage to be travelled.

We seemed to be covering about five to ten miles during darkness, which at that time of year lasted about sixteen hours.

At first I had been so excited that I seemed to be almost oblivious of weariness and cold. But after six nights on the run I became acutely aware of pain in my feet.

I tried to ignore it, but eventually I was forced to risk removing one of my canvas and rubber boots. I saw that my foot was freezing. Nothing I could do seemed to restore any life to it. I was terrified.

My hands, too, were taking on a dark tinge like deep sunburn. And I recognised the sign of exposure.

Icicles hung from my moustache and beard. My eye-lashes were frozen. Breath from my mouth condensed into snow that caked the breast of my jacket. My teeth and gums ached terribly.

But on and on we went. I knew that if I succumbed, even for a few minutes at night, to the almost overwhelming urge to rest I would be frozen to death where I lay.

Only the weak warmth of the sunshine by day saved me, bringing a little life back into my frozen, racked limbs.

And so we plugged on, night after night, with Kim slipping away occasionally by day to fetch some scraps of food. He seemed to be almost impervious to the cold. He was born and bred to it, of course, and an appallingly hard life obviously had made him as tough as leather.

At last we crawled to the top of a hill and there, about five miles away, shimmering in the crystal visibility of the eighth dawn, was the sea.

I forgot all my aches and pains. I actually leaped for joy, and, weak as I must have been, felt I could rush down and run all the way to the coast.

But soon I calmed myself and looked again. There was something odd about that coastline. It took me a long, long time to realise what it was.

Even when I knew in my own mind the bitter truth I didn't believe it—I couldn't, wouldn't believe it.

Then the realisation, and its implications came to me like a savage blow in the face.

The sea was frozen. There was solid ice for miles out into the ocean. Every boat would be sealed up in the harbours. There was no hope of escape that way.

This possibility, obvious as it should have been, had never occurred to me. I was so horrified, so utterly dejected by the discovery that I slumped to the ground and sobbed like a babe.

After a while Kim shook my shoulder, gently. He wanted to know what was wrong. By signs I explained. He simply nodded his head, sadly.

Now I had to decide what to do.

My feet were in a terrible state, but I couldn't just lie there and die.

Across country to the United Nations lines was 200 miles at least and I had no maps and no knowledge of the geography of the place.

I could give myself up to the North Koreans, but I'd heard of the merciless treatment other prisoners had received from them. At best, they would probably beat me to death.

Slowly the truth became clear to me. My choice was to die, or to get back to where I had started. In prison jargon I'd got to bug back into the place I'd bugged out of—or else !

It was almost impossible to convince Kim, who was still in fine shape, that I meant to go back. But, at last, the sailor turned his back on the sea. And we headed east.

I expected my toes to drop off at any moment. My feet were numb. I felt as though I was walking on my shins.

There was even more urgency now about getting back than there had been about reaching the coast. It was a race against time—against frostbite, hunger and death.

The journey took us about half as long again as the outward flight—about twelve days, making about eighteen in all.

I explained to Kim that if ever I sat down or fell and seemed to be unable to get up again he was to fetch someone, anyone.

But I couldn't make him understand that, while I was going through hell rather than give myself up to the Koreans, I'd rather be picked up by them, and perhaps be torn apart, than be frozen to death out there. Death by freezing was the immediate danger and that was all I had the strength to fear just then.

Undoubtedly the prison clothing and equipment saved my life. The padded, quilted jacket and trousers gave wonderful protection from the piercing, icy wind. The all-rubber boots, with canvas on the inside and the outside of the uppers, didn't save my feet from frostbite, it's true, but I do believe that they saved me from eventual amputation. The gloves, inter-lined with cotton wool, and the quilted, peaked cloth helmet, with ear flaps, were all that could be desired in the circumstances.

One of my greatest agonies came from the sweat that froze on my body inside my clothing. The pain was beyond belief.

And the fear it brought was even worse. For I had heard of Chinese soldiers being frozen to death inside their padded clothing. After running in an attack and perspiring freely they had rested and the sweat on their bodies and clothing had turned quickly to ice.

I must have presented a bizarre picture, staggering along on the ice with the front of my jacket thrown open, my chest bare. I thought it was safer that way.

Somehow I kept on my feet, moving ever slower and slower. I threw caution to the icy wind and kept going by day as well as by night. Stumbling, lurching along like a drunk, I fell time after time into the snow. Then Kim would help me back on to my feet and on we would go again. The lad never seemed to show any sign of weariness. In his little world where only the fittest survive, obviously he was accustomed to hardships incredible by our standards.

Now I was longing to get back to my tormentors! Anything, I believed at the time, was better than this.

And at last we arrived in darkness just outside the camp area.

Kim and I looked at one another. I told him to say nothing and that if anyone brought him to identify me he should ignore me: I would say that I had tried to escape alone. I didn't want him to suffer as his mother must have been suffering at that time.

Then I told him what I didn't really believe could ever come about—that if I was still around when warmer weather arrived he could help me again. Otherwise he could aid some other prisoner.

He looked at me solemnly. Then he turned quickly and walked away. I never saw him again.

I crawled down the hill to my old hut. There were no guards, no signs of life. I pushed open the door, slammed it behind me and fell to the floor.

I felt very, very happy. And I slept.

I've no idea how long I lay there. All I know is that I was awakened by an unarmed Chinese soldier I'd never seen before.

He just looked at me in a surprised sort of way, opened his hands in a gesture of bewilderment and hurried away.

A very few minutes later I was surrounded by Chinamen of all sizes and shapes, all talking at the same time, all gesticulating wildly. And then in walked my old interrogator and his interpreter.

" Where have you been ? " they asked.

" I've been for a walk."

They told me that by trying to escape I had (that old phrase) " destroyed my future." I would be severely punished.

Then they asked if I was hungry and I said : " Yes, very."

Food was produced—steaming hot soup and boiled rice —and I was left in peace to eat it. Afterwards a doctor came to treat my frozen feet.

For two whole days they left me alone—and then they let me have it.

I bent my knees to my chin and, with movements of my jaw and neck muscles, managed to free it sufficiently to be able to breathe again.

Now, instead of hoping to doze off, I had to battle against an overwhelming desire to do so.

In the evening the guards brought in a bowl containing a glutinous jellied mass of birdseed millet. It was food, I thought wryly, just fit for a chicken.

One of the guards freed my wrists, leaving my elbows still tightly bound behind me. I could move my hands close enough together to hold the bowl, but when I tried to grip it with my fingers I found they were quite lifeless.

The guards tried to force me to hold the bowl, but I couldn't. So one of them, with a big, friendly smile that I shall never forget, fed me gently like a baby with a spoon.

When I had finished, he took a very small cigarette butt from his pocket, lit it and, with another smile, put it between my lips.

After a few puffs he removed the fag end, stamped it out on the ground, put my wrists behind my back and tied them securely again.

With a slight wave, as much as to say " Cheer up, old man," he left me and the other guard followed him out.

During the night I must have moved again, for I woke up bathed in perspiration and gasping again for breath. I screamed for the guards, using the Chinese word for " Comrade " as an inducement for them to come with the greatest possible speed.

I suppose it was only an instant before the door was thrown open, but it seemed an age to me. A flashlight shone on me and I begged whoever might be behind it to take the noose from my neck at least for the night, so that I might lie there without strangling myself.

I could see now that the man who had come was the one with the friendly smile. Desperately I tried to make him help me, to play on the sympathy which obviously he had for me. I begged and implored him to undo the noose, but it was no good. He only shook his head sadly and gave me to understand that, much as he might like to, he dare not do as I asked because his officers were " bu how " (no good).

I didn't sleep that night for fear of the noose. Once or twice I dozed off in spite of myself and each time the rope about my neck brought me gasping back to consciousness. All I could do was lie there and think. And there was nothing to think about except the prospect of a couple of weeks of bondage—and what might follow, if I survived.

In the darkness, in enforced wakefulness, imagination runs riot. I nearly scared myself out of my wits that night.

Perhaps it was just as well that I didn't know at the time of the prisoner who, bound as I was, had been hung from a wall hook in such a way that if he kicked or slipped he would have strangled himself.

I didn't know, either, about yet another prisoner in bonds who had been kept standing with the noose around his neck tied to a peg in the wall—so that if he had dozed off, struggled or slumped with fatigue, he, too, would have been his own executioner.

That man was left like that for two full days and nights before they cut him loose.

A third prisoner, was bound by North Koreans and then hung from a beam for seventy-two hours by his

Street, off Piccadilly. There we would linger over wonderful meals and the most glorious wines, chosen with great deliberation.

Of course, I had to go and see the girl's father, to ask for her hand. He was a cantankerous old so-and-so who didn't approve of me at all and thought his daughter much too young to get married, although she was twenty years of age.

It was quite an interview, with the girl intervening to implore his consent. I was trying to speak all the parts, with appropriate alterations in my voice. Several times one or other of my guards peeped in through the doorway to see what all the rumpus was about. I would ignore the interruption completely and he would stare at me, wide-eyed, obviously thinking I had gone " round the bend."

It was in the middle of the marriage service that I grew tired of the whole thing. I couldn't remember the words, anyway, and decided to find some other way of passing the time.

Soon afterwards I noticed a bee entering the hut through a tiny crack near the door. Where it came from, how it survived so early in the Spring, with the snow still thick on the ground and the cold still intense though lessening, I have no idea. But there it was. I could only imagine that it was of some special breed—as must have been the great, fat house-flies that flitted about even on the bleakest of days.

The bee flew a couple of circuits of the room and crawled along a wall before disappearing into a tiny hole. A few minutes later it emerged, crawled along the wall again and departed through the crack by which it had entered. After a brief absence it came in again and repeated its previous performance precisely.

76

I was fascinated. I found myself waiting eagerly for its repeated appearances. For three full days I watched it at work. The bee was my only companion. I used to time its absences impatiently by counting and would be most upset if it was late.

One evening I was sitting on the floor waiting for my food to be brought to me. My bee had not been back for hours and I was dejected. It seemed to me that its absences were growing longer and its movements slower, as though it was very tired, or ill.

Suddenly the Chinese soldier bearing my food threw open the door and there, crawling on the plank that served as a threshold, was my bee.

My gaze was fixed on it, for I thought it was injured.

The soldier must have seen my horrified stare. He stood there, perfectly still. I looked at his face. He looked down at my bee. And then he smiled broadly as, before my eyes, he crushed it slowly, deliberately, into the wood.

I wept long and bitterly.

The guard seemed to be surprised. He undid my wrists and went away. Presently an English-speaking Chinaman entered and asked me : " What is the matter ? Why do you cry ? "

I told him all about my bee and how it had been " murdered brutally " there on the threshold while I sat bound and unable to save it.

He listened to me quite patiently and then he said :

" Like you, bees are expendable. Like you people of the Western World, bees are workers, but they are not organised and, in consequence, their work all too often is haphazard and in vain."

was banned strictly by Chinese Army rules. But, on the other hand, I suspected that this might be the sort of place, well away from everyone—even from the Army itself—to which they might send someone for the full, Oriental-style treatment. Then, with no witnesses except those directly involved and with their remarkable capacity for self-deception, they could pretend—and, I think, really believe—that it had never happened.

As it turned out, I wasn't far wrong.

But first they brought me a sort of " last supper." It was a fine meal. There were even *peeled* potatoes. And afterwards I was given a mug of green tea and a cigarette.

In the utter, heavy silence I fell fast asleep.

CHAPTER SEVEN

I WAS AWAKENED by two new interrogators, both of whom could speak English. I had never seen either of them before. They seemed to be trying to make me think they were friendly. After bidding me a hearty "Good morning", asking me if I had slept well and whether I felt rested, one of them said :

" Our comrades at the place from which you have come were in error. They made a mistake in trying to make you sign a confession as a spy, saboteur and war criminal. We know better. We do not believe that you are any of these things."

Then they added, almost apologetically : " We have some work for you to do, but as soon as you have finished it you will go to an ordinary prisoner-of-war camp where you will lead a happy daily life." They made it sound quite inviting.

" Now," the interrogator said, " Now you will tell us all about the Royal Navy. You will tell us about its organisation, about the Admiralty and all the details of the fleets in various parts of the world. You will tell us about the different types of ships and their armament. And, when you have done that, you will tell us about Naval Intelligence and how it works. Finally, you will

F

tell us about the battle strategy of British Commonwealth ships in the Korean area."

So that was it. They wanted me to turn traitor. I didn't say a word.

They added that they would give me the rest of that day to think about it. They wanted my mind to be perfectly clear, they explained, so that when we started work I would have all the facts ready to deliver to them.

They walked stiffly from the room. When they had gone I told myself: "Now you are in real trouble." Of course I couldn't tell them anything at all about what I did know. And I found some comfort in the fact that most of the information they demanded was quite beyond my knowledge.

Early next morning, back the two of them came, with guards carrying a rude wood table and some chairs. The two English-speaking interrogators sat down and directed me also to take a seat, facing them across the table.

"And so we will start work," one of them said. And then he ordered sharply: "Speak." There was no veneer of sympathy now, no suggestion of apology.

"I don't know a thing," I said.

"What do you mean?"

"I mean that I simply haven't the knowledge you seem to think I have. May I suggest that you obtain a copy of a well-known publication, Jane's 'All the World's Fighting Ships.' In it you will find most of the answers to your questions—certainly all that are available for publication."

I was trying to sound as polite as possible, but I couldn't conceal a note of impertinence in my voice.

" You are playing with words," I was told. " It is not good to play with words. You will now begin to give us the information for which we have asked."

I remember thinking how excellent was their English, though they went astray now and then on pronunciations.

I tried to explain again that I did not know of the things that they wanted to learn. I gave a detailed description of the ground covered by each edition of Jane's " Fighting Ships," and I insisted that my job in the Navy was " Information " and had nothing whatsoever to do with " Intelligence."

" Write," I was told. " Write your autobiography to begin with. Write your life story from the age of five, through your schooling, naming every school right up to the day of your liberation by the Chinese People's Volunteers."

My inquisitors pushed a pile of paper, a pen and some ink across the table. And then the two of them sat silent, staring at me.

I decided I would not be giving anything away by playing along with them, so I started to write my life story as truthfully, as accurately and in as much detail as possible. There could be no harm in that—and it might do some good.

It took me a long time. When I had finished they read it slowly and said :

" Now you will continue to write—to write of some things which you have left out. You will think back to your grandmother and to your grandfather on both your mother's and your father's sides and you will write the history of your family to date.

"You will include full details of your family's status —how much money your father earns, particulars of the furniture he owns and the house he occupies, whether he has a car and particulars of any investments. You will give equally full information about your mother, your brothers and sisters, your grandparents and your great grandparents. You will describe your close friends."

That was a tall order. I suppose I had never thought much about it before, but I was surprised now to discover how little I knew of my family history. Anyway, I stuck to the facts as far as I could (which wasn't far) and filled out the gaps with guesses and pure fiction.

By the time I had finished, my dear old father had become a millionaire, who lived in a mansion full of priceless *objets d'art*. My mother had become an ex-Gaiety girl, who still at times drank champagne out of a slipper. I had sisters who had been presented at Court and were all going to marry into the Peerage and I had brothers who were mining diamonds by the bucketful in South Africa.

An Australian Air Force officer under similar interrogation, I heard later, named Ned Kelly, the famous highwayman, as his best friend and the mythical Pilot Officer Prune as his second best. It was all the same, anyway.

Both the interrogators read my essay. Neither of them made any comments on it. And then one said :

"Now you will write out details of the organisation of the British Admiralty."

"I have told you," I replied, "that I do not know such details. I doubt if there is anyone outside London who knows them, it's such a vast and complicated affair."

"You are lying," one of the interrogators snapped at me. "You are playing for time. You do know about such things. You are a reactionary and not a friend of the peace-loving peoples of the world. You are simply being obstinate."

For twenty-four hours without a break they kept it up. Time and time again they would say, " Now you will write." Time and time again I would explain that I couldn't.

I became very weary. At last I told them impatiently that they could think what they liked. As for me, I said, I was too tired even to think. My brain wouldn't work.

" That," I was told, " is just an excuse. You will not be permitted to sleep until your work is completed."

Then the two men left me and two new interrogators took their places at the table. They carried on the cat and mouse game from where the others had left off. " You know." . . . " I don't." . . . " You must write." . . . " I can't."

Several times they told me I would get tired of the proceedings before they would. To this my answer, each time, was " undoubtedly."

Very soon I found that I had to sleep. My brain and my body had reached the stage at which it was no longer possible to force myself to stay awake. I fought hard against the urge, but I knew, without being able to do anything about it, that my head was nodding.

At last, I must have dozed off. Perhaps my head fell against the table. I don't know. But a blow in the face that set every nerve in my body jangling brought me back to full consciousness.

" It is very rude to fall asleep during a conversation," one of the interrogators remarked calmly.

I roared with laughter. Maybe I was becoming hysterical.

tormentors sought. And what little I did know I must have kept to myself for, after my recovery, they continued to grill me on identically the same subjects.

When I came round, I was alone. The table and chairs had been removed. The hut was bare.

I stretched and felt refreshed.

Outside, beneath a clear starry sky, a Chinese soldier leaned against the wall of my hut near the door. He was humming, quietly, a tuneless little Oriental ditty.

That was the only sound in my lonely, snow-bound world.

CHAPTER EIGHT

I HADN'T BEEN awake for long, looking out on the desolate landscape and puzzling over what might happen to me next, when along came the two Chinamen who had put me through my most recent grilling.

At a glance I could see that they were up to more monkey business. The bullying attitude had gone. Now they were all sugar and spice—just as though nothing had happened. The change was almost unbelievable. It made me feel for a moment as though I had been dreaming. Perhaps that was how they wanted me to feel.

"Have you had a good sleep?" one of them asked me. He was trying to sound friendly. His tone was almost wheedling. It made me shudder slightly.

I replied briefly: "Thank you. I've slept well."

"Are you feeling hungry?"

"Like hell I am."

"Pardon?"

"I am very, very hungry."

I was, too. I hadn't eaten for a long time. And I must have burnt up quite a lot of nervous energy since the last meal.

of it that I could just feel through my clothing was like a caress. I revelled and luxuriated in it like a shaggy old tom-cat before a glowing fire.

Another great joy to me was that during these periods of exercise I came closer than I had ever come during my captivity to making some sort of contact with the outside world.

It wasn't much of a link, but at least it gave me something to think about, something to watch, something to take my mind away from my own plight. It helped me a great deal in the battle I was fighting with myself all the time—the battle against self-pity and depression.

The farmhouse had several small rooms. The farmer and his family had been evacuated from those now occupied by me and my guards, but continued for the time being to live in a third room at the end of the building.

Every day I spent much of my time watching the man and his podgy little wife going about their chores and the children at play.

I tried to make friends with them. The adults ignored me completely, but the children were less inhibited. No doubt the parents had warned them against showing signs of friendship, and I think they were scared of the Chinese guards. But still the youngsters would return a wave of the hand when no one was looking. Best of all, they would smile at me. And at that time the glimpse of an open, innocent smile on the face of a child was almost as comforting to me as the sunshine.

On the day after my " holiday " was to end, the family were due to move right away from the homestead. And on the eve of their departure they held a little feast. It was a gruesome yet fascinating affair to watch.

The main dish, served with great ceremony, was boiled dog. For days beforehand the poor animal had been starved until it was reduced to a bag of skin and bones and, of course, was ravenously hungry. All the while it had been given copious supplies of water to drink. Then, shortly before the feast, it was given a huge meal of plain, boiled rice—as much as it could eat. The water, I suppose it was, caused the rice to swell and the poor brute's stomach was soon distended like a balloon.

Next it was strung up by its hind legs and the farmer hit it a mighty blow with a chunk of wood on the back of the head. Presumably it killed the dog instantly. I don't know. But immediately after that, it was decapitated and its belly was split open.

Into one pot went the whole carcass, including the skin but minus the head. Into another went all the intestines and the rice which the animal had eaten. All were then boiled thoroughly and finally were served up amidst much shouting and laughter. The whole family, even the toddlers, tucked in with great relish.

From beginning to end it was a sight which, I am sure, would have made me sick if I had witnessed it in any other circumstances. But now I found myself looking on quite dispassionately. I remember feeling surprised that I wasn't upset about it all.

It didn't even put me off my own food—meals that came up fully to the Chinamen's promise. They were good—very good. I ate as I had never eaten before ; certainly, I should think, as I shall never eat again. And though my stomach was almost as blown out as the dog's had been, I began to feel pretty good. It is still surprising to me that one's spirit can be so mercurial—that at one moment it can sink so low as to be almost crushed and yet at the next be soaring high again with hope and new resolution.

Without any reasonable excuse for it, I was full of hope again now, and I was resolving on future tactics. I had learned, by this time, not to look too far ahead. The thought of even a few hours of comparative comfort and freedom from bullying was enough to make me content. Somehow my mind simply couldn't cope with conjecture about what might happen in the more distant future. Or perhaps it was that I wouldn't let my imagination stray that far.

Anyway, I was busy just then planning in my mind a course of action that I thought might give me a few more days respite after the end of my two-day " holiday."

I had decided that I would try a little subtlety. When the bullying started again, as I was sure it would, I would pretend that I had made up my mind to co-operate, as they called it.

They wanted me to tell them about the Navy. I'd tell them, all right. I'd tell them the way the Navy never had and never would work. They'd never know any better—so I thought. I'd draw on my imagination. I'd fool them, I told myself smugly. I'd show 'em. I had it all worked out.

And so when the two interrogators returned at the end of the " holiday " I put my plan into action. After they had asked me : " Are you prepared now to co-operate ? " I played clever. I tried to make them think I was wavering. I hummed and hawed and made a great show of indetermination. And then I went on a long and emotional tirade about " you've beaten me " and " I'll talk."

" Yes, I'll change my attitude," I said. " I'll strike a powerful blow for the peace-loving peoples of the world against the warmongers."

I was quite proud of that touch about the powerful blow. It was one of their own favourite phrases and their delight at hearing it from my lips was quite ridiculous to see. I thought they were going to slap each other on the back, they were so pleased. I had difficulty in refraining from laughter.

Of course, they didn't know of my own child-like glee over the thought that I hadn't stipulated who I meant by the peace-loving peoples and who by the warmongers. That, I considered at the time, was pretty clever.

But now, with grins right across their faces, the two dreadful characters were shaking me by the hand, congratulating themselves on what they seemed genuinely to believe was my downfall, and me on what they called " saving my future." From here on we would all be friends and jolly good company, that was their attitude.

I was given a packet of Chinese cigarettes and some matches. A table and wooden chairs were brought in and there was even a cushion for me to sit on. A fire was lighted and pen, ink and paper were laid out before me.

The ruse was working. I felt that even if it didn't last, even if my trickery were revealed and I had to be punished for it, at least I might gain a few days, perhaps weeks of comparative comfort and freedom from bullying. It was worth the risk.

When we were all seated around the table, one of the interrogators told me that first he wanted me to write my life story.

"What, again?" I asked. "But I've done that for you before. Surely this isn't necessary."

"The last time you wrote, it was for our comrades far away," I was told. "We have no copy of that statement. You must write again."

I wrote again.

I wrote the whole of my life story and all about my parents and grandparents. As usual, I filled in from my imagination the parts I didn't know. When I had finished that I was so comfortable, the atmosphere so pleasant, it was all such a change that I just went on writing.

I found a match in my hand. I had just used it to light a cigarette. So now I wrote the life story of a match. I traced it all the way from a forest in Scandinavia, through all sorts of interesting adventures until the moment it curled up and died in a film star's hand at a New York night club. I got a lot of quiet amusement out of it all. I covered nearly seventy sheets of foolscap paper with my closely packed scribbling.

When I had finished, when I couldn't think of anything else to write and I had grown tired of the physical exertion of it, I handed the manuscript across the table.

One of the interrogators glanced through the pages quickly. He didn't show any signs of surprise. Perhaps he didn't understand the part about the match, or didn't notice it. All he said was:

"That's very good, very interesting. Now you will draw a diagram of the organisation of the Admiralty in London. You will make it detailed and complete. Please take your time over it to ensure accuracy. Please make yourself comfortable."

PYOKTONG . . . Part of the town was evacuated to form a prison camp

WINTER IN KOREA . . . " A silent, frozen world of nothingness "

He passed across the table a large sheet of drawing paper. I looked at it, blankly, for a long time before starting work. Of course, I hadn't a clue about the details of the organisation at the Admiralty—and still haven't. What young R.N.V.R. officer has ? I was comforted by my ignorance, as it meant I could not possibly give anything away. But how to fake the diagram these chaps wanted was quite a problem.

However, I settled down to the job and drew a magnificent family tree. I put the First Lord of the Admiralty at the top, myself low down in the bottom half, and ended up with a mythical Ordinary Seaman Bloggs, for whom I barely had room on the paper. In between came every nautical title and rank I could think of, and to make weight a few that just seemed to sound nautical.

I got even more fun out of it than I did from my story of the match. And when I'd finished I congratulated myself that it looked really quite impressive.

I was still admiring my handiwork when I had a most pleasant surprise. My taskmasters left their places at the table and walked from the room. And as they left there entered a young Chinese girl in army uniform. She sat down across the table, facing me.

From force of habit, I suppose it was, I jumped to my feet. I moved so quickly that the chair fell over backwards. I felt very foolish.

" Good morning," she said. And those were the first words I had heard from a woman's lips since I had been in captivity.

She told me to be seated. And then she said :

" There's no need for you to stand up when I enter. I know you of the West like your womenfolk to be effeminate and you treat them as the weaker sex. It is an attitude that demands consideration towards them on your part. But we women of the new China are equal with our men and consider such behaviour to be quite unnecessary, as we are all human beings."

It was quite a speech. I listened, fascinated. And I can remember every word, every inflexion of her voice, as though she were speaking to me now.

I looked at her for a long time. She was about five foot three or four inches tall. She seemed shapely enough, as far as I could judge from the curves of her quilted uniform. On her head was a soldier's padded cloth helmet, with ear flaps and a small peak. Her glistening, straight, black hair seemed to be dressed in a bob that was long enough to show just below her headgear.

Her face, I remember thinking to myself, was not unattractive in an Oriental sort of way. She had very high cheek-bones and a rather squat nose. Her eyes were almost Western, and much larger, wider than those of the typical Chinese I had encountered.

But what struck me most about her was her complexion. It seemed almost transparent . . . clear, smooth, olive.

When she spoke it was in English almost faultless grammatically, though she went a little astray on some pronunciations. Her voice was soft : her whole manner gentle.

I longed to reach out across the table and touch with my fingers the clear, fragile cheeks, the smooth, silken hair. It wasn't that the woman aroused the slightest passion in me. She didn't. But I wanted to make sure she was there and that this was not an hallucination. For she was the first, the only thing of beauty I had encountered in that dreary, ugly world.

And now she was speaking again, gently and sweetly. She was asking me how my work was progressing.

" Very well, thank you," I replied. I couldn't think of anything else to say. I thought it sounded curiously dull of me.

" Please let me see what you have been drawing," she said.

I handed over the sheet of paper. She looked at it and then, without passing any comment, she told me :

" I think it is silly of you to have endured so much hardship when, if you had behaved like this from the beginning you would have had a happy daily life and by now would have been in a prisoner-of-war camp."

She seemed to think for a moment and then she added :

" Better late than never. As soon as you have finished your work you will go to a prisoner-of-war camp to be with your own fellows. Please continue. Please write once more your autobiography."

I didn't argue. I started to write while the girl across the table sat watching. I was thinking that she seemed to be quite cultured, well educated. Her manner, her speech, everything about her was so different from the male interrogators, all of whom were obviously from peasant stock.

It didn't occur to me that the sudden appearance of this girl was part of the general plan to make me " co-operate." My mind was too occupied in gloating over the apparent success of my own scheme. Everything looked fine. I couldn't think why I had not tried some such bluff before. All sorts of wonderful thoughts came to me about being with other prisoners again.

Every hour, now, they gave me a rest period. The girl was my supervisor for half a day of each of the four during which I spent seven or eight hours writing. When she was there, she would give me a cigarette during the breaks. Her attitude towards me was rather like that of a kindly, sympathetic nurse towards a favourite patient.

It was she who read my life story when I had finished it. I watched her face closely, but I couldn't see any signs of doubt or approval. When she had finished it, she looked me straight in the eyes for what seemed an age. She didn't look so gentle now. She said :

" This does not tie up with the one you wrote before you came here."

I pointed out that, according to her colleagues, the earlier effort had been seen only by " comrades far away."

She didn't reply to that. All she said was :

" You'll have to do it again."

So I started writing once more. Fortunately, I could remember almost exactly, this time, the words of my previous essay. So at least I could be sure these two would " tie up," as she called it.

When I had finished, she read it and seemed to accept it. She did not make any comment. Without a word, she got up and left the room.

At once one of the male interrogators came in. In his hand was my make-believe diagram of the Admiralty. He looked very cross.

" You have tried to cheat and deceive the Chinese People's Volunteers," he said. " You have committed a crime by being insincere. This diagram is quite inaccurate, all wrong."

I thought " The game's up " but what I said was :

" I told you in the first place that I know little about the organisation of the Admiralty. If you know more than I do, why don't *you* draw the beastly thing."

He tore the sheet of paper into minute pieces, which he threw at me. Then he said :

" You will be given one more chance only . . . a last chance."

He handed me another big sheet of paper and I set to work. But I was beaten from the start. I'd gone into such detail in my original version and had drawn so heavily on my imagination that I hadn't a clue how to make it even begin to look the same. And I knew that, if I didn't do just that, there'd be trouble.

Each time the girl came to supervise me she would implore me for my own good to tell the truth and not try to deceive her or her comrades. She said I should realise that she knew many things about the Royal Navy.

" If that's so," I said, " tell me about these things. Perhaps you know more than I do."

Her reply was to rattle off a whole list of strengths, statistics and other information. She certainly did seem to know more than I did. And I could recognise as accurate enough of what she told me to leave no doubt in my mind that I wouldn't be able to fool her.

Her knowledge of Royal Navy matters, in fact, was remarkable. Certainly she knew more than most junior officers of my acquaintance. I thought that either she had made a long and careful study of intelligence reports or, as seemed more likely, she had been in touch somewhere, at some time, with Royal Navy personnel. I wondered whether by any chance she might have been around Hong

The interrogator stamped out of the hut. I never saw him, or any of his fellows, or the girl again.

That night a Chinese officer and one guard came to me and said "Come with."

"Where are we going now?" I asked. And I got the usual reply.

"We go to another place. It is about two miles away."

Out we went into the snow. We walked over the hills and far away. It was pitch dark and I had no idea in which direction we were travelling. I was frightened again, and very dejected—for, up to now, each move had led to some new ordeal. I felt sure this would not be an exception.

CHAPTER NINE

DARKNESS HAD GIVEN way to a cheerless dawn, and a hazy sun, floating like a toy balloon just above the horizon, was casting long, grotesque shadows among the muddle of moon-mountain hills when we came to the end of the journey.

We were on the outskirts of a large village, heading for a mud house that stood well away from the others. A Chinese soldier, with an ancient rifle slung wrong-way-up from his shoulder, stood on guard outside.

The door was open. My guard mentioned me to go inside. As I did so, I had the surprise of my life.

There, squatting almost exactly in the centre of the bare floor, was another prisoner—the first on whom I had set eyes since leaving the prisoner-of-war camp at Pyoktong soon after I was captured.

The man was dirty beyond belief. His hair hung, lank and matted, almost to his shoulders. He was pitifully thin, hollow-eyed and haggard. Obviously he had been on his own for a long time. I could tell that by the look of him—I don't know how, but one always can. I remember thinking that in appearance he resembled the Count of Monte Cristo, as the latter must have looked at the time of his escape.

It was foolish talk, maybe. But it was talk. And that was heavenly for us. Once they moved us together to another house nearby and we began to think we might be allowed to remain in one another's company.

But at last they came for me again. I was to go to "another place" that was about "two miles away." As I left with my guards I said simply :

"Cheerio. See you again some time."

"So long, I'll be seeing you," he replied. And then he added : "Don't let these bastards get you down."

That was all.

Off I went into the darkness and this time was marched only about five miles to a lonely Korean farmhouse, where I was left alone for the rest of the night with my thoughts.

A particularly evil-looking Chinaman roused me at dawn. He was small, old and had a face wizened like a walnut. He spoke English through tightly clenched lips and, with eyes that never seemed to blink, he gave the impression that he was staring straight into my mind and out through the back of my head.

His appearance was not deceptive. As I was to discover, he was in fact very evil.

"I will give you three minutes to start answering my questions." He wheezed the words out at me. "If you refuse, or try to fool me, you will suffer." He said that word "suffer" with a kind of hiss, placing much emphasis on it, as though he relished it.

I hated his guts. I wanted to kick him in the teeth. And I shouted back at him :

"You can't make me suffer any more than I've suffered already, you ******. As far as I'm concerned you, all of you, can go to bloody hell. And be damned to you."

108

He replied quietly : " You are not being brave. You are being stupid." And then he screamed at me : " Now answer my questions. Admit you are a spy."

I didn't speak. He waited for a few minutes and then he snapped :

" I will repeat the question once more. Admit you are a spy."

Still I didn't speak. He strutted out of the room to return with two soldiers carrying a table and a stool, on which he told me to be seated.

Then each of my arms was seized by one of the soldiers. My wrists were pinioned to the table in vice-like grips, the palms of my hands down, fingers and thumbs extended. Next each guard crushed the knuckles of his free hand down into the bones of the back of my hands. It was impossible for me even to twitch a finger. Standing across the table from me, the ancient interrogator pulled from his pocket a handful of slender, long spikes—sharp splinters of bamboo.

" Have you any idea what these are ? " he asked.

I didn't answer. I was petrified with fear. I couldn't have spoken a word if I'd wanted to.

" Answer my questions, or else. . . ." And he tapped the bundle of splinters on the table under my nose.

All I could do was shake my head. . . . No.

Quite calmly, quite without expression he inserted one splinter deep under the nail of the little finger of my left hand.

I remember being surprised that it didn't hurt as much as I had expected.

" Now will you talk ? "

Just then a guard called me out. He handed me an axe, pointed to a pile of logs and, with gestures, suggested that if I wanted to get warm I should start chopping.

I was still sweating nervously, but I was cold, too. So I started chopping, although my fingers were terribly sore.

When I had finished that task, another doctor paid me a visit, looked at my hands and said : " You must be careful when chopping logs not to injure your hands. See what you have done. You have run splinters down all your fingernails."

He applied some soothing ointment and bandaged me up.

After a couple of days during which no one came near me except my guards, I was awakened just before dawn by a Chinese officer. He thrust a spade into my hands and said : " Come with."

We walked perhaps half a mile up a valley and arrived at a small indentation in the hillside. There, hidden from view, we stopped. The officer pointed to the ground and said the one word :

" Dig."

" Dig what and what for ? " I asked.

" You will dig your grave," he replied blandly.

For that I was quite unprepared. I didn't move, not a muscle. I had thought of all sorts of things, including the possibility of a firing party, but not this.

" Dig," the officer said again.

I began to dig.

WEST COAST OF KOREA . . . " There was solid ice for miles out into the ocean "

". . . *The countryside was pitted for mile after mile with bomb craters* "

CHAPTER TEN

THE EARTH, THOUGH clear of snow, was still in the grip of
winter. It was as hard as iron, rocky—tough going. I
worked steadily, but not hurriedly. My mind was awhirl.
I couldn't decide whether to press on with the job and so
get over as quickly as possible whatever was coming to
me, or to try delaying tactics with the idea of postponing
what seemed likely to be the end.

Almost subconsciously I chose a middle course. I
remember thinking that, if I had to die, it would be better
to be beneath the ground than to lie out in the open as a
feast for the Korean hogs and dogs.

It must have been a bizarre scene. In that lonely valley
hidden away among the craggy hills somewhere, I knew
not where, in North Korea there were only the two of us :
the impassive Chinese officer urging me on with a loaded
revolver pointed at the middle of my back and myself,
thin, haggard, long hair and beard flowing in the bitter
breeze, straining at what apparently was my last task.

During a pause to straighten my back I asked the
officer :

" What's all this in aid of ? "

" Dig," he said.

H

So I dug again. And for three days I dug. At the end of that time I had made only a shallow, oblong trench.

I wasn't very frightened. I couldn't convince myself that I was going to die just yet. In fact, I had almost made up my mind that the whole idea might be to frighten me into making a dash for freedom. Then the Chinaman would consider himself justified in shooting me down, and I would be off their hands—silenced, dead. I would never be able to tell of what I had experienced at the hands of his compatriots.

The Chinese had a curiously twisted morality in these matters. Just as the torturing of prisoners was strictly prohibited by their army rules but nevertheless in special cases was carried out assiduously behind the scenes and in circumstances which allowed them to delude themselves that it had never happened, so I felt certain they would be happy to shoot down a prisoner after forcing him into a situation that would give them the chance to say : " It was his own fault."

I tried to find out what the officer was up to. Walking back to the hut after the third day of digging, I attempted to make openings for a conversation. Although he had said little to me except the word " Dig," I laid on a little flattery.

" You speak remarkably good English for a Chinaman," I said.

" I ought to speak good English," he replied. " I was educated at Cambridge University."

The words came as a shock out of all proportion to their significance. They infuriated me. I could put up with this sort of treatment from the Chinese—just about—but there was something dreadful about the idea of a " Cambridge man " being involved in it.

114

And anyway, I didn't believe him. That made me more furious still, foolishly furious. I remember thinking that no Cambridge man would blow his nose with his fingers as this chap did, frequently.

I shouted at him : " That, like everything else you Chinese say, is obviously a damned lie."

He shrugged his shoulders, gave a stupid little giggle and said nothing.

At once I was sorry I had lost my temper. I wanted to find out more. When I had calmed down, I questioned him. I asked him what year, which college, about any contemporaries. But he acted as though he didn't hear me.

I studied him more closely now. He was tall for a Chinaman, tight-lipped, thin, and his eyes were even narrower than usual. His nose was particularly prominent and big. His air was haughty, nonchalantly arrogant.

He wore spectacles and, I noticed now, had a habit of continually pushing them higher up the bridge of his nose with the second finger of his right hand.

Obviously he was accustomed more to city streets than this boulder-strewn countryside. He walked daintily, carefully picking his way. He made me feel clumsy as I clobbed along beside him in my big, ill-fitting, rubber boots.

Several more times on the way back I tried to make him talk to me, but he wouldn't.

That night I lay awake for a long time trying to decide whether there could be any truth in what he had told me. I think I was battling against allowing myself to dwell on the forlorn hope that, if he really had the background he claimed, I might just conceivably be able to persuade him to help me in some way.

Next morning, when the self-styled "Cambridge man" appeared at my hut, I held out my hand for the shovel as usual. But he hadn't brought it with him. We walked without it to the grave.

There he took out his revolver. Keeping well out of arm's reach he covered me with it and said :

"Kneel down."

I didn't move. He waggled the gun at me. So I knelt at the edge of the grave.

As I have said before, I have great faith in my convictions. At that moment I was still not convinced at all that I was about to die. Still I wasn't frightened. I remember thinking that perhaps the "Cambridge man" was making a final effort to induce me to run for it, so that he could shoot me down. I couldn't believe he would kill me cold-bloodedly, without excuse, like this.

Watching him carefully, not missing a thing, I saw him empty the cartridges from the chamber of the revolver and then replace one, putting the rest into his pocket.

Then he spun the chamber with the palm of his hand, closed the weapon and walked slowly in front of me and around to my back.

I heard some more clicking which, I thought, could be either the hammer being pulled back to the cocked position or a cartridge being taken from or put into the chamber. I didn't know which.

From the corner of one eye I saw the revolver coming around my head and then felt the touch of the barrel just behind the temple.

So this devil was going to play the game called Russian Roulette with me.

116

I remembered tales of how Russian soldiers and occasionally (usually in drink) British Servicemen gambled their lives in this suicidal game. They would place one cartridge in a six-chambered revolver, spin the chamber, put the barrel to their heads and squeeze the trigger, having betted money, and their lives, on the chance that the cartridge was not in the chamber opposite the hammer.

All this I remembered in a flash as I realised that the spinning chamber of the Chinaman's gun was to be my wheel of fortune. I was frightened, now, all right!

I knelt there motionless as I heard and felt the slight creak of the trigger being squeezed.

There was a dull thud that pounded in my brain.

Was that what it felt like to be shot in the head? How should I know? I didn't even know at that moment whether I was alive or dead.

Slowly I put my hand to my temple. God alone knows what I expected to find. But there was no hole there. I could scarcely believe my sense of touch. It meant I must be alive.

I turned to look at my captor. He was staring down at me impassively. He put the cartridges back into the chambers and said "Get up." But I found I couldn't move. He helped me to my feet.

Much later that day I calmed myself down and began to think coherently again. I convinced myself that the whole affair had been a hoax, that there had never been any possibility of my being shot . . . that the cartridges must have been removed behind my back.

That was a conviction that comforted me on each of the six other mornings in succession on which the whole performance was repeated.

By the seventh morning I was so cocky about the whole thing that I greeted the officer with a hearty "Good morning." And on the way to my grave told him:

"I do appreciate this morning walk. It's the only exercise I get all day."

But as I stood up after the usual ceremony, he said:

"Wait. You think I have been playing games with you. Watch this."

He turned away, extended his right arm and squeezed the trigger of the revolver.

There was an explosion. And a bullet whined away off the icy ground.

The walk back to my hut that morning took much longer than usual. Now my mind was tormented by doubts. Obviously I could not face another morning walk to the graveside with equanimity.

All night I lay thinking, working myself into a fever of dread. Sleep, the comforter, deserted me this time.

And then it was dawn. I waited for the "Cambridge man." He didn't come. A silent guard brought me some food, and still I had not been called out. I waited all day, all night and the next day. But I never saw him again.

For a whole week I was left alone, sometimes in a cold perspiration from apprehension, sometimes full of optimism. Now there were not even any more interrogations— nothing, except doubts.

No one came near me at all except the guard, who shoved my meals through the door of the hut in which I was kept locked.

By Chinese standards I was well fed. I was given rice and flat, thick rounds of baked dough, like Indian chapattis. Potatoes boiled in their skins were also provided. And even without the necessary salt they tasted very good to me. But perhaps my greatest joy was the clean hot water I was given to drink instead of the greasy stuff, like washing-up water, to which I had become accustomed.

During the whole of that week I was never once allowed to leave the hut for any purpose. The place began to stink abominably and I was worried again by thoughts of disease.

Day after day I paced up and down the length and breadth of the place, and then from corner to corner, like a caged animal. There was nothing else to do—except sleep, in which I luxuriated for seventeen or eighteen hours out of the twenty-four.

Loneliness, I think, was now the greatest burden to bear. I had no news at all of the progress of the war, and I began to wonder how long I could remain sane in my solitude; whether I was doomed to this for always; whether I would ever again enjoy the society of people of my own kind.

For a while I became convinced that the war had ended; that I was a forgotten man; the last, lost United Nations prisoner in North Korea. It was a terrifying idea. I had to fight it, hard.

At other times I found myself trying to imagine what else the Chinese might do to me in their attempts to break me down. Some pretty horrifying thoughts came to me. I wasn't so very worried about tortures, but I developed a phobia about being slowly starved to death locked away in some God-forsaken spot like this until I rotted.

So the soldiers picked the thing up themselves and heaved it into the cart. For ten minutes or so they laboured at their self-imposed task while I stood looking on. And then they told me to climb aboard again.

Perched on top of the stolen timber, I was carried now through the first truly beautiful scenery I had seen in North Korea. Unlike most of the countryside through which I had passed, the hills here had not been stripped of trees. They were densely wooded, lovely to look at. And, now and again, great fat pheasants would wing their way across our path.

Each time that happened the guards would look round towards me with wide grins, stick their thumbs in the air and say :

"Choppa, choppa—Ding how," meaning "Food— Good."

They seemed to be almost as pleased as I was to be among these hills after the dreary desolation of the other places. They began to sing a Chinese song. I roared out "There's a long, long trail awinding. . . ." It was like an August bank holiday outing.

After what must have been about twenty miles, the cart stopped and I was told to get down from it. A Chinaman walked along the road towards me. I recognised him as an English-speaking guard I had encountered very soon after my capture.

"You have taken a long time to get to a prison-camp area," he remarked. "Where have you been ? "

"On vacation," I told him facetiously.

Then he pointed to what seemed to me to be an ordinary, large Korean village.

" This is where you will remain," he said. " See all those houses. Every one contains prisoners."

" What's the idea of shutting them up in a place like this ? " I asked.

" They are all prisoners who would not co-operate," he replied. " They are serving gaol sentences for misbehaviour."

Good God ! I thought. What new horror is this ?

There was something eerie about the village. No one was to be seen in it except a Chinese soldier standing on guard outside each doorway. The only sound on the air was the shrill song of a bird somewhere in the distance. My heart began to pound. The hairs at the back of my neck were tingling ; perhaps they were standing on end.

I didn't like the look of this at all.

one another's company. Even while we harboured such doubts and suspicions, each secretly brooding on them, we were overjoyed to be able at least to talk to someone— someone of one's own kind—if only about generalities.

One of the first things I learnt from the American was that this village we were in was close to a place called Pyongjang-Ni, east of Pyoktong, where I had spent those early days in the prisoner-of-war camp. Now I knew, for the first time, that all my travels about North Korea had brought me nearly full circle to where I had started off.

Well, at least it was good to know roughly where one was. It helped to dispel that feeling of being utterly lost.

The American told me, too, that here we were in what the Chinese called a " first class " or " number one " gaol. It was the best thing of its kind to be found outside the P.O.W. camps and some of the prisoners, it seemed, were allowed to live together in groups of from two to twenty or more.

Best of all was the news that we came now under " semi-lenient treatment policy." In theory, this meant that we would be allowed to write and receive a few letters from the outside world and would be given a ration of cigarettes or tobacco and matches, a little sugar, reading matter, tooth brush and paste, a tiny cube of sickly-sweet scented soap and other small " comforts."

It seemed too good to be true. But, sure enough, along came my reading matter. It consisted of books like " War and Peace," " Silas Marner," " Pride and Prejudice," " A Tale of Two Cities," " Oliver Twist," the complete works of Pushkin, Stalin and Lenin and some translations of contemporary Russian and Chinese best sellers. The selection obviously had been carefully made with the idea of furthering political ends.

I was also given pen, ink, paper and envelopes, but though I wrote many letters, none was ever delivered and neither did I receive any mail. My American friend was more fortunate. He heard that some of his letters had got through and calculated that he received about one in every ten sent to him.

My first smoker's ration consisted of a tiny quantity of small tobacco leaves. With it came a sheet from an old Chinese newspaper which I was instructed to tear into strips to form cigarette papers.

Smoking now became a matter to which we devoted considerable study and much ingenuity.

The Chinese newspaper, we found, made the best cigarette papers because it burned comparatively slowly and gave off a lot of acrid smoke. But when we hadn't got any, the American would read once again slowly and carefully, memorising every word, one of his treasured letters from home. And then we would tear that up into strips.

His wife no doubt would have been bitterly hurt if she had known how I cursed her, at times, for using expensive, thick notepaper that was so unsuitable for cigarette rolling. About once a month, however, my companion received a letter from an aunt in Ohio, I think it was. She used very thin and very satisfactory air-mail paper. How I loved that woman.

Every cigarette butt and every scrap of ash we saved in a little cloth bag. And then, when our tobacco ration had been consumed, we would smoke those leavings. Sometimes we would add a few dried pine needles, rolling up the whole horrible mess into a cone like a firework. It tasted like hell, but the more we coughed and spluttered the more we joked and enjoyed ourselves.

127

All the events of which I have written up to now occurred during a period of less than four months—about 120 days.

Never once in that time had I been able to take a bath or wash my body. I had washed my face and hands only on three occasions and my hair had been cut once by a Chinese soldier. I was crawling with lice. Filth was caked on the inside of my clothing. My beard had grown long and was flowing wildly. I must have presented a dreadful picture.

Running hard by our hut now was a babbling brook. Crystal clear water danced along with a merry gurgling sound. And one day we were allowed to go to it.

The temperature of the water was just above freezing point, but we both decided to take a bath. We stripped off our clothes, gasped at the iciness as we dipped our feet, and then went splashing and floundering out into midstream, getting as wet as possible as quickly as we possibly could.

We actually turned blue with cold, but oh, the joy of it ! Afterwards, having put on our padded trousers and jackets, we washed our revolting shirts and underpants and romped about like children on the bank of the stream.

In one way and another, the American and I managed to get a good deal of fun out of life in a simple way.

Having companionship at last, and with the knowledge that other prisoners were in the houses all around us, we became quite " cocky " and, egging one another on, made the lives of our guards as miserable as we could without bringing trouble on our own heads.

Every time one of them opened the door to see what we were up to we would roar at him : " Get to hell out of here," and tell him in several languages that he was " bu how " (no good).

130

When we were ordered to sweep the courtyard every morning we refused, saying we had not dirtied it as we were never allowed out.

"Let the Koreans sweep it. They use it," we said.

That line worked wonders. Our guards let us out into the courtyard for one hour each day and from then on each morning we swept the place clean.

There was a strict rule that prisoners must not sing. But we sang at the tops of our voices, night and day. And the more our guards screamed at us to stop, the more noise we would make.

The American had not been able to carry a tune in his head and so, note by note, I taught him all the songs I knew. We used to joke about how surprised his kids would be, when he got home again, to hear him singing "Rule Britannia," of all things.

As the days passed and our cheekiness increased, so our morale soared. We were amazed and delighted to find just how much we could get away with, taking it as a sign that the Chinese believed the war was coming to an end.

Frequently, now, we would make the rudest of gestures at our guards. They were furious at first, but didn't do anything to stop or punish us. In the end they became so accustomed to it all that they would make the same gestures back at us.

We became almost arrogant, at times, but always with the sobering thought at the back of our minds that probably this was too good to last.

One of our biggest triumphs just then came when we won the confidence of the Camp Commander's father-in-law, an old boy who seemed to be acting as nursemaid to his daughter's five-year-old child while that good lady carried out her duties as Political Commissar of the district.

During our hours of exercise we often saw the little girl playing in the village and would wave to her. At first she wouldn't take any notice of us, but after a while she began shyly to wave back.

Always we would point to ourselves, stick our thumbs in the air and indicate, by mime, that we were jolly good, first-rate, number-one fellows.

One day we were delighted to see the child, walking past accompanied by grandpa, raise her little thumbs and evidently tell the old man that we were jolly good, first-rate, number-one fellows.

He smiled at her, then at us. And at once we asked him for some tobacco. He looked around, smiled again, and then handed us a plug of good, strong, wonderful stuff. He often gave us a smoke as he passed by after that.

Another big occasion was that on which a young Chinese soldier on guard outside the door of our house so far forgot himself as to pass the time by cleaning his ancient Japanese rifle and actually taking the bolt to pieces.

For the life of him he couldn't get it together again. We watched his bewilderment for some time and toyed with the idea of making a dash for freedom while he was disarmed, but decided it would be worse than useless to make a break without proper preparation.

After a while, the American winked at me and then, by signs, made the guard understand that he could fix the rifle for him. Without a thought, the boy handed it over, complete with the magazine full of cartridges.

My companion busied himself for some time getting the bolt together again. At last he pushed it home, tested the trigger pressure and made a slight adjustment. Throughout these operations the Chinaman looked on calmly, without a care in the world.

Suddenly the American pulled back the bolt and pushed it home again, thus putting a cartridge " up the spout." Then, pointing the weapon to the sky, he squeezed the trigger. There was a loud report. The Chinaman nearly jumped out of his skin. And the American shoved the rifle back into his hands.

In next to no time, Chinamen were running in our direction from all quarters. The American, in a remarkable piece of comic mime, let the soldier know that he was to say he had dropped his own rifle and that was why it had gone off. Then we stood back nonchalantly and waited for the fireworks.

An excited officer was first on the scene. Soon many other Chinamen gathered around, all talking at once. And our poor little guard, not daring to admit he had handed over his rifle, had to say the whole thing was his fault.

His explanation seemed to be accepted, for in the end the crowd dispersed, and the three of us were alone again.

The American was delighted. Then he put his fingers to his lips in the gesture of a man enjoying a cigarette and held out the other hand, palm upwards.

The soldier looked at the American, then at me, and finally in the direction of the departed visitors. Slowly he took from his pocket a packet of cigarettes, extracted two and held them out to us.

The American shook his head and indicated that he wanted the whole packet. The guard handed it over without a murmur.

Every morning after that, as soon as the guard appeared, the American demanded a packet of cigarettes, making it quite clear that unless he got it he would tell the officers how he had been handed the rifle.

In the end the wretched Chinaman used to hand over the packet—probably his entire daily ration—as soon as he arrived and without being asked for it. We felt so sorry for him that sometimes we would give him back two or three cigarettes. That delighted him enormously.

On one occasion we carried our insolence just a little too far. We were particularly rude to a Chinese officer who came to visit us. We refused to stand up when ordered to do so, flung at him every kind of British and American abuse of which we could think, and behaved generally in the most boorish manner imaginable. It was too much for him.

" I can see," he said, " that these conditions are too good for you. I will see that you are punished."

We laughed in his face. And we continued to laugh when the guards marched us off and locked us up in a shed only three feet wide and ten feet long.

There we found that both of us couldn't lie down to sleep at the same time chiefly because at one end there was a large hole from which a huge rat would emerge at night to nibble at anyone nearby. So we had to take our rest in turns.

For five days we were locked up in that little shanty without ever being allowed out—not even to go to the latrine. We were so cock-a-hoop, however, that we managed to keep on laughing and joking and singing.

But in the end the stench of our own filth became almost unbearable. And we decided to raise hell.

First we yelled and screamed and set up the very devil of a din. We heard some guards running up, but they just stood outside chattering and didn't seem disposed to let us out. Probably they thought we had gone mad.

So next we took a flying run at the wooden door and kicked a plank clean out of it. There was more commotion outside and soon we heard the voice of an English-speaking Chinaman.

" Silence ! " he screamed, and added something about damaging the people's door.

" Let us out of here, you bastard," the American replied.

" You have damaged the people's door," came the voice again.

This time the American made quite a memorable little speech.

" If you get me a people's ruddy hammer and some people's ruddy nails, I'll fix the people's ruddy door," he shouted. " But if you don't get us out of here in a hurry there's going to be plenty damage to a coupla pairs of the people's pants. Get us out of here, damn you."

To our surprise, the door was opened a foot or two, a pair of arms came through the opening and the American was hauled out with a jerk. I tried to follow, but three or four Chinamen put their shoulders to the door and slammed it closed against me.

I yelled blue murder, and kicked and pounded at the door. A Chinese soldier shoved his rifle, with bayonet fixed, through the gap where the plank had been kicked out. He waggled the weapon about blindly, trying to drive me back.

With my boot I managed to wedge the rifle between the door and the wall. And then I unfixed the bayonet, which I shoved backwards and forwards through the hole in the direction of a pair of Chinese trousers I could see on the other side.

That caused a fine old commotion. There were yells and sounds of more footsteps racing towards the shed. Whoever had been hanging on to the other end of the rifle suddenly let go and it fell with a clatter to the ground.

"Look out," I shouted, "I'm coming out fighting."

I took a flying run at the door, caught it squarely with my shoulder and it flew open.

Thinking about it now, I suppose I should have expected to be shot dead at that moment.

Instead I saw a little half-circle of Chinamen, standing wide-eyed and open-mouthed well back from the doorway. They just stared at me, like so many wooden soldiers.

I stopped in my tracks, picked up the rifle and then, holding the weapon by the barrel in one hand and the bayonet by the point in the other, I said :

"If you lead me to the lavatory, you can have these back."

A Chinaman said in English :

"Stand to attention. I am an officer."

I had such a stomachache that I couldn't have stood to attention if I had wanted to. I could barely stand still.

"I don't give a damn what you are," I replied. "I am a British officer, but I still have to go to the lavatory."

They led me to the lavatory. It was a little cubby-hole of a place with a roof so low that I couldn't stand up. I was kept locked in there for the next 12 hours.

Soon after this incident we were back in our old house and had settled down to sleep one night when an officer walked in and said :

" Bring all. Come with. You go to nudder place."

We were surprised, and a little anxious lest we should be separated after nearly two months together and returned to solitary confinement.

" All right," I said, " but give us a light so that we can get our things together."

The " things " consisted chiefly of bits of rag, precious paper for cigarette rolling, a pack of cards we had managed to blackmail out of a guard who had been unwise enough to agree to play a game with us, and a few odds and ends such as the snake skin.

" No light," the officer replied.

" No light, no come with," I said. " Buzz off till morning and then we'll be delighted to accompany you."

The man became quite angry and the guards did a bit of rifle rattling, so we decided to obey. Groping around on hands and knees, we collected everything we could find and then followed the officer out through the door.

He led us through the centre of the village, where there was not a sign of life except for the guard at each door. It was pitch dark and we couldn't see far around us, but we sensed we were skirting a ridge that we had been able to see near the centre of the place in daylight.

Just when we felt certain that we were heading out of the village, our escort stopped outside a house and pushed open the door. The guard who was on duty there shone a light inside and we saw that we were joining two more

137

prisoners. Both were United States Air Force officers, Lieutenant-Colonel Gerald Brown and Major David Macghee.

I did not know either of them, but they had heard of me. As soon as the officer had gone and the guard had shut the door, Major Macghee said :

" Where the hell have you been ? "

And as I told him (none of us was so alarmed now about " canaries "), I discovered that it was quite well known among many prisoners that a young British naval lieutenant had been getting what they called the " run around." Via the " grape-vine," through information passed on by other prisoners who had caught sight of me when I had thought I was quite on my own, and from scraps of loose talk wheedled or blackmailed out of Chinese guards, quite a lot about my movements had become known to other prisoners. And it was then that I discovered there were many others being moved around the country, as I had been, from one place of solitary confinement to another, but not with such secrecy as their captors imagined.

The guard, hearing our murmuring, poked his head around the door several times to order us to sleep, but we sat in the darkness and talked the night through. The Major, we heard, had been given a very rough time early in his captivity. The Colonel had suffered a lot of solitary confinement, but no physical punishment.

The four of us remained together for about four weeks. Eight hours a day, every day, we played bridge. The Lieutenant and I finished up 75,000 points down—at a mythical dollar a point. The rest of the time, when we were not sleeping, we either talked or sang.

The singing was taken very seriously, in American glee club style. Colonel Brown, a happy, tubby little man, used to be quite carried away by his own fine renderings of the folk songs. And we would sit enthralled, listening to his songs like the one about :

> " In the evening by the moonlight
> You can hear the darkies singing."

Then one morning an officer came to visit us. He paced up and down for a while, just staring at us, before he said :

" I am the officer in charge of daily life. Of course you have noticed how good your living conditions are here. This is a first-class gaol to which you have graduated. The Camp Commander is very pleased that you have been giving no trouble. He has decided to move you to join a larger group of prisoners, so that you will have an even happier daily life."

" Fine," we chorused. " When do we go ? "

" Tomorrow," he said.

So bright and early next morning we had all our possessions packed ready to move and, sure enough, off we went. We walked through the village for the first time in daylight, waving happily to prisoners we saw on the way, and came to a long, low house which, we found, already had fifteen other inhabitants.

I was overjoyed to find among them three Commonwealth prisoners—the first I had encountered. Two of them were South African Air Force Lieutenants and the other was Flight Lieutenant " Butch " Hannan, of the Royal Australian Air Force.

Hour after hour, day after day, " Butch " Hannan and I talked of things that only the British can discuss— cricket, rugger, soccer, pubs, beer, darts and things like that. It gave each of us a new lease of life and we were as happy as anyone could be in the circumstances.

139

As had happened in the prisoner-of-war camp the year before, our gaolers here went out of their way to help us to celebrate the occasion. They gave us a lot of extra food— more than we could eat, in fact—a bottle of beer each, and extra cigarettes and matches.

We managed even to secure permission for one prisoner dressed up as Father Christmas to take small gifts, contributed by all of us from our rations, to the five or six men we knew to be in solitary confinement in the village.

We drew lots for the job, and one of the South Africans got it. Late on Christmas Eve, off he went, with a small sack of gifts on his back.

We waited impatiently until he returned. And then the story he told reduced us all to silence, if not close to tears.

He described how he had knocked at door after door and opened it to see the solitary occupant lying cold, dirty, wretched on the floor. He spoke of the light that had come to those men's tired eyes as they had seen him, a symbol of happy Christmases past, standing at the threshold. And he depicted for us the child-like delight over the pitiful little gifts he bore.

When the South African had stopped talking, it was a long time before anyone spoke, or moved.

With Christmas behind us, " Butch," Joe and I really got down to the job of planning the escape. I was the only one who had made a " break " and the other two were eager to learn from my experience.

They readily accepted my advice not to make the attempt in winter time. We decided to go in the early summer, when the weather would be kind and crops would be growing in the fields to feed us.

142

CHAPTER TWELVE

EARLY IN THE new year, Hannan, Ryan and I spent a great deal of time playing cribbage, the object of many of the games at first being to decide who should undertake various chores such as water carrying, yard sweeping and so on. The prize, paradoxically, was usually even greater idleness than that already forced upon us.

Soon, however, the gatherings became less innocent and more purposeful. Now they were simply a convenient cloak for detailed planning of the escape which the three of us had decided to make together.

Hour after hour, day after day we discussed every conceivable aspect of the project. We tried to visualise every possible obstacle and hazard and devise a means of overcoming each. Everything any of us had ever heard or read or experienced of life in Korea, about the technique of escape and the routine and habits of the Chinese and North Korean armies—every scrap of knowledge was pooled and, if possible, put to use in the formulation of our scheme.

I believe the idea of the three of us making the break together was mine originally, though the others readily agreed with my arguments in favour of a joint effort.

My theory was that two or three heads working together at the problem of outwitting the enemy would have far tighter would be the security arrangements and the greater the risk of capture.

Eastwards to the sea would be a very long trek—at least 200 miles, we believed. It was wild, rugged country, sparsely populated and, we reckoned, unlikely to contain many soldiers. Food probably would be unobtainable *en route*.

My own fancy was to head north, crossing the river into Manchuria and then strike west to the top of the Yellow Sea. I believed that if we were picked up, wearing P.O.W. uniforms, by the Chinese in Manchuria we would simply be interned. If we were captured on the run in North Korea, on the other hand, either we would be torn apart by the wrathful Koreans or we would be tortured in punishment by the Chinese. But I couldn't convince my companions that the Chinese in Manchuria would be sufficiently honourable or conventional simply to intern us.

In the end, after weighing up all the risks we could imagine, we decided to go east, strike the coast and put to sea. We knew that there were some large fishing craft up there, manned chiefly by aged Koreans. We would watch and wait for our chance to shanghai one of them and then sail either due south, making a landfall south of the 38th parallel, or else clear across the Sea of Japan.

With the idea of benefiting by the best of the weather and getting food from the fields wherever crops might be growing in that desolate part of the country, we planned to leave not earlier than mid-June and not later than mid-August.

Such was the secrecy with which we worked on our scheme that our plans were well advanced before we discovered that other prisoners also were making ready to escape during the

146

fine weather in two groups, one of two South Africans and the other of three Americans.

That was a complication as, of course, it was not inconceivable that the plans for two or more " breaks " might clash to the extent of causing complete failure for all concerned. Besides, it seemed likely that after one escape the security regulations might be tightened up so much that others would find it impossible to get away.

So now we set up an escape committee to co-ordinate the various plans and decide how we might all succeed.

Quickly we came to the conclusion that the only hope lay in a mass break, with all of us getting away at the same time but immediately splitting into three groups to head in three different directions, thus (we hoped) confusing our hunters.

As to the means of escape, Chris Lombard, a South African Air Force lieutenant who had been a miner, suggested a tunnel and everyone agreed that it was a good idea.

Under the floor of our hut there was a space of about two feet between the floorboards and the ground. We decided that we would dig there and tunnel our way fifteen or twenty feet to emerge outside the wattle and barbed wire fence of the compound.

Only two of us could work under the floorboards at the same time : one digging with our only implement, the head of an old Korean hoe, and the other dragging away the dirt in an old gunny sack and piling it up towards the corners of the building.

Working in shifts of up to two hours at a time, it was a gruelling and nerve-racking task. Above us the other five would-be escapers kept guard, forming a chain of communication from the courtyard to the centre of the hut.

147

Our escape group decided that, when the time came, we would slip off during one of these recreation periods into a field of maize that was growing tall beside the school-yard. It was a slender hope, as we knew that our absence would be noticed almost immediately. But it seemed to be the only chance and it would be up to us to outwit our pursuers once we had set out.

Now we began to save scraps of food and bits of cloth for use as bandages if we should be injured. We feigned sickness, particularly bowel trouble, in order to secure a few sulphur tablets. And we pretended headaches and toothaches to get supplies of codeine.

Pieces of steel were ground down to form knives and thus generally we fitted ourselves out with escape gear. We secreted it carefully to evade regular searches of the whole place and of every man. When the time came for the first escapes, the Americans failed to find a suitable opportunity and so forfeited their priority. Now it was up to us.

It was the first week in July and we had one week left before we were due to set out. And at that point Hannan and Ryan were both suffering from raging toothache. They were almost demented with pain.

The Chinese first aid man offered to try and pull out the offending teeth and both men readily agreed. Hannan's tooth broke in the process, however. His gum became infected and his cheek was so swollen that it seemed likely to burst.

With time running out on us, I agreed to wait until Hannan was fit to go and both of us urged Ryan to push off on his own.

That afternoon I walked with Ryan in the march to the playing ground, leaving Hannan lying on the floor of the hut, writhing in agony.

150

Surreptitiously, as he thought, Ryan slipped into the maize while I kicked up a fuss to distract attention to the other end of the ground.

One of the sentries who, I am certain, had not seen anything of the disappearing act, seemed to sense something was wrong. He half walked and half ran to the very spot where Ryan had slipped into the corn and presumably caught a glimpse of him on the run.

He shot the bolt of his rifle, putting a round " up the spout." I held my breath, waiting for the bang. Other guards went running up, all making ready to shoot.

I closed my eyes, unable to bear the sight of what seemed to be the inevitable slaughter. But Ryan, a soldier of many years' experience, had weighed up the situation. He knew it would be suicidal to go on and so, after about sixty seconds of " freedom," walked slowly back into captivity.

He was taken away to solitary confinement, where he remained for the rest of the war.

A week later, Hannan's face was better and we were preparing to make our break when we learned from the English language news sheet which the Chinese were giving us at the time that negotiations for the ending of hostilities in Korea were " nearing the final stages."

We decided that never had a man suffered a more timely toothache. We realised that, but for it, we might have been on the run out in the blue, suffering all sorts of unpleasantness, at the very time the war came to an end. And in all probability we would not have known of it.

Two weeks passed and no news came except that Syngman Rhee, the South Korean premier, had released thousands of Korean prisoners, a move which we expected to gum up the whole affair and which made us wonder seriously whether we had been foolish not to carry on with our escape plan.

In fact, at this time we were still expecting that in the end we would have to make a break for it. We couldn't trust what the Chinese told us or believe that the negotiations would succeed.

Then one morning we were told to assemble for an address by the Camp Commander. We sensed that this was no ordinary talk. And we hoped against hope.

We gathered together in complete silence, having agreed that, whatever it was the Chinaman was going to tell us, we would show no signs of emotion at all.

The Commanding Officer strutted up and spoke quickly, in a high-pitched voice, a few incomprehensible sentences. An interpreter repeated them in English.

"Armistice." That was the only word we heard. Our hearts leaped. But still no one moved or made a sound.

The Camp Commander seemed unable to believe his senses. He stared at us for what seemed to be a long time. Then he turned and started to walk quickly away. But before he had gone far he stopped and looked at us again, as though doubting whether we had understood.

Major Jimmy Wilkins of the United States Marine Corps, a devout Roman Catholic, stepped forward and motioned to us to remove our headgear. And then in a clear, steady voice he started the prayer . . .

" Our Father, which art in heaven . . . "

Every man took it up. I have never heard a prayer uttered so devoutly, so fervently. And the end of it, the silence was almost painful.

Then the Camp Commander wheeled on the Captain, shrieking at him in Chinese. The interpreter asked : " Why did you step out of line without permission ? "

" I am a Christian," the Captain replied fearlessly. " We are all Christians. We were offering our thanks to our Lord and Maker for the ending of hostilities."

He was marched away and thrown into solitary confinement.

We all walked slowly, silently, back to our schoolhouse and it was only when we were sure we were not being observed that the hand-wringing, the back slapping and the leaping for joy began.

Almost at once we were moved to join about 100 other prisoners in the large schoolhouse down the road and were told that we were to be sent south the following morning.

I tried to temper my joy with thoughts of the Chinese threat that I might never leave North Korea, or that if I did I would be the last to go. It was difficult, but I was frightened enough to succeed—up to a point.

I watched the trucks arrive. I noted all the preparations for the move. But still I hung on to my doubts—just in case. I was actually sweating coldly, with misgivings and apprehension.

And that night there was a torrential, blinding rainstorm. Water swept down from the hills in torrents and carried away the bridge we were to have crossed.

The Chinese soldiers set to work at once, piling rocks across the stream to make a ford. We offered to help, but they wouldn't let us. So for two days we sat and watched them. It seemed like a month.

At last they got the trucks across. We waded up to our chests through the torrent. It must have been an amazing sight. The thin line of haggard, dishevelled men, many with long beards flowing in the breeze, struggling through the water towards freedom.

Aboard the trucks, heading north-east, we sang and shouted and laughed as we dried our drenched clothing in the breeze. For many of us the laughter was the first for many months, even years, that was not a trifle forced. For all of us the singing seemed as rousing as any grand opera finale, the shouting as carefree as any from a football ground grandstand.

We knew we were being taken to a place called Kaesong where, if all went well, we would be handed over to our own people. Many of us suspected that the process of release from captivity might not turn out to be so straightforward as the Chinese were making out, but just then we did not let our minds dwell on the possible snags. These moments were too golden, too joyous to be spoiled.

After nearly twelve hours of jolting and jerking along over atrocious roads, we reached the railhead at a place called Nampo. And there we were herded into tumbledown boxcars which, to judge from the stench of them, had been occupied recently by Korean hogs.

By now the singing and shouting and laughter had died down. We were tired, and the reaction to our early excitement was setting in. We began to express doubts about the sincerity of Chinese intentions. Sitting there in the darkness of the filthy trucks, we gave way a little to gloom.

We had been told that the rail journey to Kaesong was no more than 250 miles. But days and nights dragged by— and still we had not reached our destination.

During the second day we saw clearly why we were proceeding so slowly. On both sides of the single-track line, the countryside was pitted for mile after mile with bomb craters. And the farther south we travelled towards the front line the more damage there was.

Towards the end of the journey, there was barely a square yard of ground within two or three hundred yards of the railway that did not bear evidence of the intensity and accuracy of the United Nations bombers.

Some of the craters had smooth, symmetrical sides. That was where a single bomb had landed. Many others, however, were fantastically shaped, with uneven, jagged edges. Those were the spots which had been blown up more than once. It was as though some fearful, subterranean upheaval had struck this long, narrow strip of terrain. More than anything else it reminded me of artists' impressions I had seen of moon-mountain country.

To add to the scene of chaos, the wreckage of hundreds of trucks and many locomotives lay in wild confusion alongside the track. Most of them were just twisted, almost shapeless masses of metal and splintered wood. Others were peppered with holes from machine-gun and cannon strafing.

In the valleys and on the beds of streams and rivers that we crossed was the wreckage of bridges. Our train crawled cautiously over temporary viaducts crazily constructed from tree trunks and boulders.

Everywhere there was a tangled steel jungle of weirdly distorted railway lines. And as we approached Pyongyang, the North Korean capital, the rusty hulks of United Nations and Russian tanks and lorries lay among the wreckage.

Three days and three nights had passed when we were ordered out of our trucks, which by now were more evil smelling than ever. It was a joy to be out of them and to feel the fresh, clean air on our filthy, bearded faces as we were driven off in Russian-built lorries.

We were being taken now from end to end of Pyongyang, through the heart of the capital. It was a dead heart, one that long since had ceased to beat.

Now no one laughed, no one sang, no one shouted. The sight of the place reduced the heartiest and most callous among us to shocked silence.

To hate and despise our captors, to goad and torment them—that was one thing. But to revel over what had befallen them here—that was quite another.

"Serve them right, the bastards," an American near me muttered. I looked into his eyes and thought he did not believe what he said.

"Christ!" a tough Australian said.

That was all. No one else uttered a word. Or, if they did, I didn't hear them.

The city had ceased to exist. It was completely flattened by bombing. But, in spite of this, it was still thickly populated. Some of the people were living in shacks built from rubble. Others appeared to emerge like rats from holes in the ground.

As we drove along the tracks that once had been streets, the Koreans watched us go. They were as silent as we were. They stood in little groups—just gaping, with that strange blankness peculiar to Orientals.

If they hated our guts, they didn't show it. If they were glad the war was over, they didn't show that either. They just stared as the convoy rumbled along. And we stared back.

We came to a river that runs through the city. And there we saw why we had been transferred to lorries. The great railway bridge had been broken so many times by bombs that trains only of two or three trucks could cross it. We crawled over a patched-up road bridge and, on the other side, were herded again into dirty boxcars.

Thus we continued to Kaesong, where more lorries were waiting to take us to a place about five miles outside the town, to a hillside covered with tents. Here we were to await our turns for repatriation. And while we waited I had time again to brood over the Chinese threat that, if I left North Korea alive, I would be the last to go.

It had not been held over me recently. There had been no hint or sign that it would be carried out. But I couldn't forget it. Try as I might to banish the fear from my mind, fight as I did to introduce cold reason to the arguments that kept churning around in my brain, somehow I sensed instinctively that my captors were planning to keep their word.

Our arrival at the hillside camp increased the number of prisoners there to about 700. We were allowed to mingle freely, and we spent much of our time seeking news of friends and acquaintances we believed to have been in captivity.

Every evening we all assembled to listen, with bated breath and pumping hearts, as an English-speaking Chinaman read out from a typewritten list the names of the men to be handed over the next day. Then the fortunate ones would be showered with congratulations from the rest of us, their backs would be numbed by hearty slaps and their arms almost pumped out of their sockets in handshakes. But usually they were too dazed with joy to know what was happening to them.

And so the next evening would come around . . . another list . . . the same electric atmosphere . . . the droning of the Chinaman's voice . . . more congratulations.

For those of us who were to stay it seemed almost unbelievable that, within hours, these few fortunate ones among us would be eating Western food ; sleeping in beds between clean, white sheets with pillows for their heads ; perhaps drinking a glass of beer ; going to the toilet without having to ask permission ; strolling in the open air without armed guards ; talking to whom they wished about anything they chose ; singing any song as loudly as they liked. It seemed unreal that they were actually about to experience that precious thing which ordinary folk treat so casually—freedom.

But perhaps tomorrow it would be our turn. Or would it?

Day after day for three weeks I waited like that. More prisoners arrived from time to time. Most of them stayed a while, and then passed on. Still my name was not called out.

Now only about twenty of us remained in the camp and there were no more new arrivals. The evening lists became shorter and shorter. The tents were being pulled down. Obviously we were the last prisoners remaining in Communist hands.

One day we were told to get into a lorry. Our hearts leaped with excitement. But instead of going south we drove only a short distance to a building on the outskirts of Kaesong. Our guards told us we would be moved again next morning.

Were they going to carry us off, back into the wilderness of North Korea ? We did not know. We hardly dared to wonder.

At dawn they came for us again. And this time they took us to an old Buddhist temple. Our dejection was complete.

But, after twenty-four hours there, a Chinaman appeared. He was carrying a sheet of paper. We were to be handed over to the United Nations in two groups, he said.

He read out the names of those in the first group. Each man, as his turn came, climbed abroad a lorry that stood nearby, with its engine running. When it went trundling away I looked around me and counted seven other prisoners.

Two hours passed. Another lorry appeared. The Chinaman walked up with another sheet of paper. I looked at the lorry. Its engine was idling. I toyed with the idea that, if my name was not called out now, I would wait until the others were aboard and then leap into the driving seat to make a dash for it.

The Chinaman began to read the names. He did it with great deliberation. Five times he spoke. And then he stopped. He looked calmly at the two of us who were left—the last two prisoners in North Korea.

And then it came ... "Lieut. Lankford, British Navy ... Lieut. Costello, British Army."

The two of us jumped into the lorry and away it went.

Soon we saw a bridge ahead. At one end there stood a Chinese soldier; at the other a giant American military policeman. There was a wide grin on his weather-beaten face as he waved us a welcome. I doubt whether I smiled back at him. I think I just stared.

Around two bends in the road and there it was—a brightly coloured arch bearing in huge letters the three words

WELCOME TO FREEDOM

EPILOGUE

A question I am often asked, and one which I often ask myself, is why the Chinese ever released me to reveal what I suffered at their hands.

One reason, I think, is that United Nations Intelligence left them in no doubt that evidence existed to prove I was an unreported prisoner. Another, maybe, is that the Chinese, with their capacity for self-delusion, clung to the simple belief that if I lived to tell this tale I would not be believed.